HUMAN EXCELLENCE AND EDUCATION

HUMAN EXCELLENCE AND EDUCATION

Edited by

Dr. S.K. Panneer Selvam

Assistant Professor

Deptt. of Education

Bharathidasan University

Tamil Nadu

(India)

DISCOVERY PUBLISHING HOUSE PVT. LTD.

NEW DELHI-110 002

Published by:
Tilak Wasan

DISCOVERY PUBLISHING HOUSE PVT. LTD.
4383/4B, Ansari Road, Darya Ganj
New Delhi-110 002 (India)
Phone : +91-11-23279245, 43596064-65
Fax : +91-11-23253475
E-mail : parul.wasan@gmail.com
discoverypublishinghouse@gmail.com
web : www.discoverypublishinggroup.com

First Edition: **2013**

ISBN: 978-93-5056-269-7

Human Excellence and Education

Printed at:
Dynamic Printers
Delhi

Preface

Our human brain is incredibly capable, when it comes to taking a huge amount of data and quickly digesting it and coming up with the one best solution. This is good, when it comes to making quick decisions in emergencies and under time pressures. Unfortunately, making quick decisions can often deprive us of arriving at more effective, long lasting determinations. We are often too ready to accept a solution that seems to work, rather than the truly creative solution. The latter provides a sort of exhilaration. It is contagious. Once employees are involved to this degree, it is hard to turn back. You may have heard the classic tale of two siblings who argued over who would get an orange. They compromised and split it in half. One ate half and threw away the peel; the other, who was involved in a cooking project, grated the peel and discarded the rest. Compromise is good, especially when one considers the alternative, but creative or interest-based negotiation can provide much greater satisfaction. Negotiating is the process of communicating back and forth, for the purpose of reaching a joint agreement about differing needs or ideas. It is a collection of behaviors that involves communication, sales, marketing, psychology, sociology, assertiveness and conflict resolution. A negotiator may be a buyer or seller, a customer or supplier, a boss or employee, a business partner, a diplomat or a civil servant.

Negotiation is so important for personal and business success; it is rather surprising that most people do not negotiate very well—judging from their performance in realistic business negotiation simulations. The dramatic instances of lose-lose outcomes, the winner's curse, walking away from the table, and the agreement bias raise the question of why people are not more effective at the bargaining table if negotiation is indeed critical for business success. The reason is not due to a lack of motivation or lack of intelligence on the part of negotiators. Many of the managers who fall victim to the major sins of negotiation do so for three primary causes: absence of feedback, satisfying, and self-reinforcement. A pervasive belief is that good negotiation skills are something that people are born with, not something that can be readily learned. This is false because most excellent negotiators are self-made. In fact, there are very few naturally gifted negotiators. We tend to hear their stories, but we must remember that their stories are *selective,* meaning that it is always possible for someone to have a lucky day or a fortunate experience. An interesting exercise is to ask managers and anyone else who negotiates, to describe their approach to negotiating. Many seasoned negotiators believe that their negotiation style involves a lot of "gut feeling," intuition and "in-the-moment" responses. We believe that this type of intuition does not serve people well. Effective negotiation involves deliberate thought and preparation and is quite systematic. The goal of this book is to help managers effectively prepare for negotiation, become more self-aware of their own strengths and shortcomings, and develop strategies that are **proactive** (*i.e.,* those that anticipate the reactions of their opponent) rather than **reactive** (*i.e.,* those that are dependent upon the actions and reactions of their opponent). Thus, excellent negotiators do not rely on intuition; rather, they are deliberate planners.

Education plays a dominant role as an effective instrument for large scale achievement and revolution in all spheres. Purposeful education enables the individual to understand and study the real life situation and to develop an opportunity for creating confidence in the minds of younger generation, and provide a strong base for rational and value-oriented and nation building progress. 'Humanities' courses in higher education play a significant role in this context. Therefore, a close introspection of the trend of humanities courses in higher education is essential; not only for making them attractive, but also in shaping them to be socially relevant, obviously, the courses in humanities are considered non-utility-oriented subjects, whereas they involve heavy cost to the exchequer. Many recent world developments similar to those that have produced the existing approaches to peace education have been articulated as human rights issues and problems, so that some peace educators are adding human rights to the list of approaches.

While the addition is certainly necessary, it is far from deficient and fails to exploit the essential contribution that human rights can make to peace education, namely providing the basis for a prescriptive, holistic yet particularized approach that would make peace education not only more comprehensive but also far more comprehensible. The actual human experiences that comprise much of human rights education are more readily understood than the theoretical and analytical concept of peace education. The originality of this edition owes to the contributors. As an editor I acknowledged to the contributors.

Dr. S.K. Panneer Selvam

Contents

Preface

1. **Deteriorating Trends in Humanities Courses 1**
2. **Determining the Human Excellence 5**
3. **Cultural Relativism and Universal Human Rights 9**

Cultural Relativity — Defining "Cultural Relativism" — Relativity and Universality: A Necessary Tension — Human Mechanism — Cultural Variation — Categorical Cultural — Significance of Cultural Values — Importance of Relatives — Rhetorical Devices — Moral Values of Human Rights — Varieties of Cultural Relativism — Evaluation of Cultural — Relativism in Implementing Human Rights — Conception of Human Rights — Universal Rights — Culture and Relativism — Argumentative Cultural — Other Views — Justification of Cultural — Assessing Claims of Cultural Relativism — Human Rights — Recent Trends in Women's Rights — Conclusion.

4. **Human Rights Education in UN Peace Building: Form Theory to Practice 26**

UNTAC's Human Rights Education Mandate and Strategy — Formal Education — Informal Education — Conclusions Lessons Learned — References.

5. **Human Rights and Cultural Values 49**

Caste in India — Caste and the Contemporary Struggle for Human Rights.

6. **Human Rights as Education for Peace** 68

Peace Education Needs Human rights education—Development Education—World Order Studies—Environmental Education—References.

7. **Human Rights, National Security and Terrorism** 88

8. **Essentials of Negotiation** 93

The Mind and the Heart—Negotiation as a Core Management Competency—Dynamic Nature of Business—Sidebar 1-1. New Businesses and Careers—Interdependence—Competition—Information Age—Diversity—Most People Are Ineffective Negotiators—The Major Sins of Negotiation—Why are People Ineffective Negotiators?—Absence of Relevant and Diagnostic Feedback—Satisficing—Self-reinforcement—Debunking Negotiation Myths—Myth 1: Good Negotiators are Born—Myth 2: Experience is A Great Teacher—Myth 3: Good Negotiators Take Risks—Myth 4: Good Negotiators Rely on Intuition—Learning Objectives—The Mind and Heart.

9. **Interpersonal Negotiation Skills** 105

Prepare —Search for Clarity—Show Patience—Maintain Integrity—Avoid the Presumption of Evil—Control Emotions—Understand Time Pressures—Break Down Bigger Issues Into Smaller Ones—Separate Problem from Self-Worth—Avoid Threats and Manipulative Tactics —Focus on the Problem Rather than the Solution—Try for Interest-Based Solutions —Admit Error and Apologize —Reject Weak Solutions —Be Tentative About Reading People's Feelings—Summary—A Final Note—References.

10. **Managerial Negotiations** 133

Is Negotiation Necessary?

11. **The Mind and the Heart** 142

Negotiation as A Core Management Competency—Dynamic Nature of Business—Sidebar 1-1. New Businesses and Careers—Interdependence—Competition – Information Age – Diversity – Most People are Ineffective Negotiators – The Major Sins of Negotiation – Why are People Ineffective Negotiators? – Absence of Relevant and Diagnostic Feedback – Satisficing – Self-reinforcement – Debunking Negotiation Myths – Myth 1: Good Negotiators are Born – Myth 2: Experience is A Great Teacher – Myth 3: Good Negotiators Take Risks – Myth 4: Good Negotiators Rely on Intuition – Learning Objectives – The Mind and Heart.

Index **155**

Deteriorating Trends in Humanities Courses

Education plays a dominant role as an effective instrument for large scale achievement and revolution in all spheres. Purposeful education enables the individual to understand and study the real life situation and to develop an opportunity for creating confidence in the minds of younger generation, and provide a strong base for rational and value-oriented and nation building progress. 'Humanities' courses in higher education play a significant role in this context. Therefore, a close introspection of the trend of humanities courses in higher education is essential; not only for making them attractive, but also in shaping them to be socially relevant, obviously, the courses in humanities are considered non-utility-oriented subjects, whereas they involve heavy cost to the exchequer. As a result, the teaching fraternity lacks motivation and tends to inculcate a dull and non-pragmatic sense of stagnation in their pursuits.

In India, there are about 234 universities, 39 deemed universities and scores of institutions of national importance. The total number of colleges is 9703 with an intake of 6.755 million students taught by 32 million teachers. The University Grants Commission has approved 119 autonomous colleges of which 44 are in Tamil Nadu, 38 in Madhya Pradesh, 19 in

Andhra Pradesh, 5 each in Orissa and Himachal Pradesh and 2 each in Maharashtra and in Gujarat. In Tamil Nadu, there are 385 arts and Science colleges, in which 60 are government colleges, 133 aided colleges and 192 self-financing unaided colleges in 1999-2000.

In 1999-2000 out of 4, 01,631 students 94,540 took up BA courses, 24 percent were in humanities, 40 per cent in science and 18 pursue red B.Com courses in Tamil Nadu. The humanities caption now includes subjects like history, economics, geography, Political science, public administration, psychology, journalism, adult education, anthropology, demography, tourism and literature.

A Close introspection of the date on the performance in examination reveals that the pass percentage is higher in unaided colleges as they cater mainly to the elite class, who pay high fees. The next category is aided colleges that cater to the middle and upper middle classes who pay moderate fees and, the last category is the government colleges as this segment caters mainly to the poor classes with minimum fees. Obviously, unaided colleges close the humanities sections in courses as they are commercially unviable and some colleges close the sections in course humanities of time. Government and aided colleges on the other hand have mostly the humanities courses in the regular stream. Generally, students come to college without aim and some more attend classes for scholarship sake only. This tendency exists only in south Indian University Campuses. Of course here, the reason for the prosperity of the humanities courses is the existence of enormous facilities like scholarship, sponsorship, placement and avenues for vertical and horizontal mobility. Again the craze for joining these courses in the northern universities and colleges is also mainly due to the prevailing atmosphere for an easy access to get selection in the all India Competitive Examinations. Another reason for the sharp fall in the strength of humanities is also the availability of such courses through the centers of distance education.

The following are some of the considerations that students opt for humanities courses. The mushrooming matriculation schools provide jobs for graduates and the fees for science education courses are higher, and it is easy to pass a humanities course. While medicine and engineering courses are popular among students, the mediocre students opt for science courses and the dull profile students ultimately select humanities courses. Post graduates courses like law, management or making courses are neither attrition do they assure a white color job. The science graduates take up job generating courses or computer oriented courses. The teachers of humanities courses are also partly responsible for this deteriorating trend. The Board of study in the university does not generate on the job and off the job training facilities to suit the changing scenario and requirements of society. Nor are there any practical training classes, or field visits or in plant training modules for the humanities courses.

The teachers and students mostly rely on ready-made guides. The teachers do not update themselves or publish articles and hence fail to deliver lectures on new things that emerge. The students also notice this lack of constant up graduation on the part of the teachers. The teachers also fail to utilize modern teaching equipments effectively. The media broadcast of the Mass contact programmes does not attract students. The students manage to get cent percent in internal assessment and also distinctions in the university examinations. The aptitude for research comes down for want of suitable employment and, ghost, writing and plagiarism are on the anvil. The M.Phil. programmes are unattractive and poised for a natural death. The universities and integrated study programmes, the guest lectures, inter collegiate lectures, youth exchange programmes, should be included more often in the college manifesto.

The training method for teachers are conventional and old fashioned and is mere liability items in colleges. Teachers are reluctant to pursuer research in the absence of pecuniary benefits. The libraries are no longer the temples of learning. The journals have to be purchased. By coordinating with proper guidance and leadership programmes it should be possible to harness the potential of the students of humanities to become responsible citizens.

The deteriorating trend of humanities courses in the campuses can be averted and proper structural changes implemented. Dual degree programme, additional course programmes, computer literacy drive for arts students, Star status for institutions should be the ultimate success inputs that one must think. The students are to be trained as per social needs. Cost effective, socially beneficial training schemes may be taken up to popularize the humanities courses. Campus selections of the best student will also motivate the participants to reap the right harvest. The crisis management strategy may be dispensed with and efforts must be made to attract the volatile strength. A long-term planning is essential to strengthen the do or die exposition of the humanities courses in future.

Determining the Human Excellence

Indian schools and teachers should come out from their tunnel vision of conventional; teaching, Indian organizations have already started adopting many manufacturing and technological inputs from abroad. To match these things, Indian schools and college should also concentrate on such ideas as multiple intelligence and Neuron linguistic Programming at the school level. We are at the end of this millennium looking forward to the expectation and excitement the next millennium is going to offer. Lot of changes has taken place leading one to guess the type of changes that are going to take place in the next century. The world has become very competitive. The competition has also ushered in huge opportunities for anyone who is willing to prepare oneself to exploit the same. In this context, the issue of preparing our students to meet the challenges of the next millennium becomes very critical. The approach to education and personality development has taken a very different dimension during this century. Parents dimension during this century. Parents are very keen to make their children assume greater responsibilities in their lives. Great emphasis is given for imparting quality education for their wards. The single purpose of education and curriculum development can only be towards preparing the student to partake in the excitement of the next century.

World over, the emphasis on education has been shifting from not only academic excellence but also to overall excellence. In this context, the concept of Multiple Intelligence is very crucial, to meet the challenges of change, children should be developed in various parameters. Lot of research has taken place in understanding the human excellence. The Brain which is come the center of command for the human system has been studied from various perspectives. One of the researchers is Dr. Howard Gardener, who has done extensive research on human excellence. He defines intelligence as "the ability to solve problem that counters in real life and the ability to generate new problem to solve". He says the human mind should also have the ability to make something or offer a service that is valued within one's culture. He focuses of eight types of intelligences:

(i) Linguistic intelligence: It is the ability of a student to express ideas and concept in words. Communication is going to play a very vital role in the years to come and students should be in a position to express them clearly and succinctly so that they are able to convert their knowledge into usable products. Students who have high level of linguistic intelligence perform very well as writer, speakers and journalists.

(ii) Logical Mathematical intelligence: It is the ability to concentrate on mathematical problems, hypotheses and to think logically. Scientists, accountants, engineers, computer programmers, researchers all have a high level of this intelligence.

(iii) Spatial intelligence: This is a very important skill which will enable a person to think in a three dimensional perspective. It calls for a high level of visual constructed images and creativity in oneself. Student with spatial intelligence have the capacity to become architects, painters or pilots, which call for this skill in the day-to-day application of their work.

(iv) Bodily-kinesthetic intelligence: This intelligence is the ability to manipulate various things and objects. It also calls for fine tuning physical skills; one would appreciate the extent to which athletes and sportspersons, dancers or surgeons.

(v) Musical intelligence: The brain has two halves *viz.*, the left hemisphere and right hemisphere. The left hemisphere is logical, mathematical and linguistic. On the other hand, the right hemisphere is the hemisphere where the music and creativity talents are developed. Students who have a high degree of musical intelligence are high brain driven. These students demonstrate their ability to understand and contribute to music. They can appreciate the parameters such as pitch, melody rhythm or tone. The students who excel in this become leading composer's music directors, music critics or instrument makers. If this intelligence is developed among students, their right brain is activated and they start thinking creatively.

(vi) Inter-personal intelligence: This is the capacity to improve the rapport and people manage skills. In the life of anybody, whatever may be the intelligence and knowledge; if one cannot connect with others they will not be very effective. In this context, inter-personal intelligence becomes very important students who excel in inter-personal intelligence to go as teachers, social workers, politicians or nay one who has to interact with public at large.

(vii) Intra-personal intelligence: It is the ability to introspect and understand oneself in newer dimensions. It also includes the ability to plan ahead and direct one's life students with a very high of intra-personal intelligence are able to understand their strengths and weaknesses. Student who have this ability become theologians, psychologists, philosophers or original thinkers.

(viii) Naturalist intelligence: It is the ability to understand nature and use the gifts of nature for one's own development. Students with high level of naturalist intelligence of well as agriculturists, farmers, landscapers, etc. It is possible in an educational institution to develop the above eight types of intelligences. With the unfolding of the next century, the opportunities are going to be very wide. In our country, we have been seeing excessive importance in certain disciplines such as engineering, medicine and computer programming.

The world offers equal scope and opportunities in other fields also. For example, there are not many writers, architects, original thinkers or scientists. With the economic reforms and liberalization of the Indian economy, the migration of students to various parts of the world has becomes very common. This means that the students have to be prepared not only for the Indian requirements but also to the world requirements.

India is witnessing the entry of multinational organizations. To succeed in the future business environment is going to be a difficult ball game. If the students are not developed properly to meet the challenges of change, it is going to be very difficult for them to compete in the newly changes order. Many research and application based books are available to develop Multiple Intelligence in a classroom situation. Applying Multiple Intelligence and Neuron Linguistic programming skills in a classroom makes a lot of difference in the quality of life and capabilities of the students. Indian school and teachers should be able to come out from their tunnel vision of conventional teaching Indian organizations have already started adopting many of the manufacturing and technological inputs from abroad.

To match these things, Indian schools and colleges should also concentrate on such ideas as Multiple Intelligence and Neuron Linguistic programming at the school level. If this is not donning, Indian students will be left behind in the march towards the next millennium in which all other countries are going to participate.

Cultural Relativism and Universal Human Rights

Cultural Relativity

Cultural relativity is an undeniable fact, moral rules and social intuitions evidence an astonishing cultural and historical variability. The doctrine of cultural relativism holds that at least some such variations cannot be legitimately criticized by outsiders. But if human rights are literally the rights everyone has simply as a human being, they would seem to be universal by definition. How should the competing claims of cultural relativism and universal human rights be reconciled? I defined an approach that maintains the fundamental universality of human rights while accommodating the historical and cultural particularity of human rights discussed above.

Defining "Cultural Relativism"

What we can call radial cultural relativism would hold that culture is the sole source of the validity of a moral right or rule. Radical universalism would hold that culture is irrelevant to the validity of moral rights and rules. Which are universally valid? The body of the continuum defined by these ideal typical endpoints—that is, those positions involving varying mixes of relativism and universalism—can be roughly divided into what we can call strong cultural realism and weak cultural relativism.

Strong cultural relativism holds that culture is the principal source of the validity of a moral right or rule. Universal human rights stand, however, serves as a check of potential excess of relativism at its furthest world extremes, just short of radical relativism, strong cultural relativism would accept a few basic rights with virtually universal application, but allow such a wide range of variation for most rights. Those two entirely justifiable wets might overlap only slightly. Weak cultural relativism holds that culture may be an important source of the validity of a moral right or rule. Universality is initially presumed, but the validity of human nature, communities, and rights serve as a check on potential excess of universalism. At its furthest extreme, just short of radical universalism, weak cultural relativism would recognize a comprehensive set of prima facie universal human rights, but allow occasional and strictly limited local variations and exceptions.

We must be careful not to use merely quantitative measures of relativism; qualitative judgements of the significance of different cultural variations must also be incorporated. In a rough way, three-hierarchical levels of variation can be distinguished, involving cultural relativity in the substance of lists of human rights, in the interpretation of individual rights, and in the form in which particular rights are implemented. As we move "down" the hierarchy, we are in effect further specifying and interpreting (in the ordinary sense of that term) the higher level, and the range of permissible variation at a given level is set by the next higher level. For example: "Interpretations" of a right are logically limited by the substance of a right; even the range of variation in substance is set by the notions of human nature and dignity from which the list of rights derives. I shall ultimately define a weak cultural relativist position that permits deviation from universal human rights standards primarily at the level of form.

Relativity and Universality: A Necessary Tension

The dangers of the moral imperialism implied by radical universalism hardly need be emphasized. Radical universalism is subject to other moral objections as well. Moral rules, including human rights, function within a moral community. Radical universalism requires a rigid hierarchical ordering of the multiple moral communities to which individuals and groups belong. In order to preserve complete universality for human rights, the radical universalism must give absolute priority to the demands of the cosmopolitan moral community over all other ("lower") moral communities.

This complete denial of national and sub-national ethical autonomy and self-determination is not acceptable. Even if the nation should prove to be a doomed, transitory stage in the development of human moral community, there is no inescapable logical or moral reason why people cannot accept or choose it as their principal form of social organization and the locus of important extra familial, moral and political commitments. Similar arguments might be made for other communities that do not encompass the entire human race. Once we allow the moral validity of such commitments, we are bound to accept at least certain types of substantive moral variability, including variability in human rights practices. Such moral "nationalism" may be based on political reasons, such as an inability to agree on the structure of a supranational organization, or a fear of creating an instrument of universal tyranny. More directly moral reasons might also be advanced-for example, the advantages of international diversity provided by a strong commitment to national or local customs. Most important, it resets on the notion of self-determination. However, it is justified, as at least certain choices of such moral communities demand respect from outsiders—not necessarily uncritical acceptance, let alone emulation, but in some at least, tolerance.

If radical universalism cannot be justifiably maintained—at least with respect to any robust substantive list of human rights, such as provided in the at Universal Declaration and covenants—even a weak cultural relativist account of human rights seems on its face guilty of logical contradiction. If human rights are based in human nature, on the simple fact that one is a human being, than how can human rights be relative in any fundamental way?

Human Mechanism

The simple answer is that human nature is itself in some measure culturally relative. There is a sense in which this is true even biologically—for example, if marriage partners are chosen of the basis of cultural preference concerning height, weight, hair color, skin tone, or other physical attributes, the gene pool in a community may be altered in ways that are equivalent to "natural" mechanisms of selection. More important, culture can significantly influence the presence and expression of many less easily quantified aspects of human nature—for example, by encouraging or discouraging the development or perpetuation of certain personality traits and types.

Cultural Variation

Whether we conceive of this process as involving cultural variation around an unalterable core or as cultural variations largely within a physiologically fixed range, there is a social side to human nature that cannot be defined, at least insofar as that nature is expressed. "Human nature" is a range of possibilities varying, in part in response to culture, within certain psychobiological limits; it is as such a project and an individual and social discovery as it is a given fact. Even if all behaviour should prove to be ultimately genetic, the expression of that genetic endowment in human behaviour—which also merits being called "human nature"—is in considerable measure culturally determined.

Categorical Cultural

The strongest form of radical cultural relativism would hold that the concept "human being" is of no moral significance, that the mere fact that one is a "human being" is irrelevant to one's moral status. Many premodern societies have not even recognized "human being" as a descriptive category, but instead defined persons by social status or by group membership. For example, the very names of many cultures mean simply "the people" and their origin myths may define them as separate from outsiders, who are somehow "not-human." Similarly, the ancient Greeks divided the world into Hellenes and barbarians.

Significance of Cultural Values

Even more striking is the apparent cross-cultural consensus dense on a few practices that cannot be justified by even the hoariest of traditions, and certainly not by any few customs. For example, the prohibiting of torture and the requirement of procedural due process in imposing and executing legal Punishment seem to be accepted as binding by virtually all cultures, despite profound differences in specifying the practical and substantive meanings of these notions. There is also a striking cross-cultural consensus on many of the values that today we seek to protect through human rights. Especially when those values are expressed in relatively general terms as Life, social order, family, and protection from arbitrary rule, and prohibition of inhuman and degrading treatment, the guarantee of a place in the life of the community, and access to an equitable share of the means of subsistence are central moral aspirations in nearly all cultures.

Importance of Relatives

The radical relativist might respond that such consensus is irrelevant. Logically, this is correct; cross-cultural consensus does not necessarily entail any additional force for a moral rule. But most people do believe that such consensus adds force to the rule. So this kind of radical relativism, although logically impeccable, is in an important sense morally defective. In effect, a moral analogue to customary international law seems to operate. If a practice is nearly universal and generally perceived as obligatory, that practice is required of all members of the community, it would impose certain substantive limitations on the range of permissible cultural moral variation.

Rhetorical Devices

Plausible arguments can be advanced to justify alternative mechanisms to guarantee human dignity – for example, nature law, which imposes Tran cultural moral obligations that are not correlative to right. Few in any state, however, actually advance such arguments. In the first, second, and third worlds alike, a strong commitment to human rights is almost universally proclaimed, even where practice throws that commitment into question. And even if such proclamations are mere rhetorical fashion. Such a widespread international moral "fashion" must have some substantive basis.

Moral Values of Human Rights

That basis is the moral hazard presented by the modern state. Traditional rules usually faced substantial moral limits on their political power, customary limits that were entirely independent of human rights and the relative technology and administrative weakness of traditional states and non-state political institutions further restrained arbitrary abuses of power. In such a world, inalienable entitlements of individuals held against state and society might plausibly be held to be superfluous, if not positively dangerous to well-established practices that realized a cultural conception of human dignity.

Such a world exists today only in a relatively small number of isolated areas. And the modern state, particularly in the Third would, not only operates relatively free of the moral constraints of custom but also has far greater administrative and technological reach. It thus represents a serious threat to basic human rights seem necessary rather than optional. In contemporary circumstances, then, radical or universe rifted relativism, is as inappropriate as unrestricted universalism. Some kind of intermediate position is required.

Varieties of Cultural Relativism

(a) Internal versus External Judgments: This distinction between internal and external evaluations roughly corresponds to, and further elaborates, the distinction between strong and weak cultural relativism; the stronger one's relativism, the greater one's reliance on internal evaluations. It also helps to elucidate the dilemma we face in judging culturally specific practices, torn between the demands of relativism and universalism.

Respect for autonomous moral communities would seem to demand internal evaluations, but to rely on internal judgment alone abrogates one's moral responsibilities as a member of the cosmopolitan moral community. Membership in one's own national or local moral community might also demand judgment. Furthermore, moral judgments are by their nature universal, or at least universalizable, even we know that moral values and particular judgment are at least in part historically specific and contingent.

Evaluation of Cultural

The choice between internal and external evaluations thus is itself a moral choice. Should we abandon an external judgment because a practice has a long and well-established place within another cultural tradition? Our answer to that question should depend in large measure on the moral importance of the practice, from both the external and the internal perspectives, and on the nature of the internal judgment.

We can identify the force underlying such judgment is the inherent universality of basic moral precepts, at least as we understand mortality in the west. We simply do not believe that our moral precepts are for us and us alone. This is most evident in Kantian and other deontological moral theories, but it is no less true of utilitarianism; the principle of utility is explicitly advanced by Bentham and Mill as a universal moral principle. And, of course, nature of human rights theories is also inherently universal. For most of us, morality is inherently universalitistic and egalitarian.

Futhermore, our moral precepts are our moral precepts. As such, they demand obedience of us. To refuse to act on our own precepts simply because others reject them is to fail to give proper weight to our own moral beliefs, at least in the case of central moral precepts, such as the equality of all human beings and the protection of innocents. And no matter how firmly someone else, or even a whole culture, believes differently, at some point we simply must say that those contrary beliefs are wrong. Negative external judgment may be problematic, but in some cases at least they seem not only permissible also demanded.

Relativism in Implementing Human Rights

The distinction between variations in form and in interpretation may be difficult to draw with precision, but it is fairly clean and important. Consider a particular right, such as the right to political participation. In further specifying the right to political participation, we can begin by distinguishing electoral from no electoral, from non-electoral forms of participation. Within the realm of electoral participation, we can distinguish elections based on universal adult suffrage from those based on a suffrage limited by sex, income, or some other such criterion; elections where voting is a right from those where it is a privilege or even a duty; elections intended to determine the will of the people from elections that serve principally to mobilize popular support for government policy, and so forth. These variations in "interpredation" clearly are qualitatively different from questions of "form" such as how often elections, town meetings, plebiscites, or gatherings of village elders will be held they shall be called.

Conception of Human Rights

Particular human rights are likely "essentially contested concepts" in which there is a substantial but rather general consensus of meaning coupled with a no less important and apparently irresolvable conflict of interpretation. In such circumstances, culture provides one plausible and defensible mechanism for selecting interpretations. Nonetheless, there are strong limits on the acceptable range of variation. Not all "interpretations" however, are equally plausible or defensible. They are interpretations, not free associations or arbitrary stipulations. The meaning of—"the right to political participation," for example, is controversial, but the range of controversy is limited by the substance of the concept: an election in which a people were allowed to choose an absolute dictator for life is simply an indefensible interpretation. Furthermore, even logically valid interpretations are more subject to external criticism than variations in form.

When such priorities are set, an especially extreme emphasis or de-emphasis of aright brings us to the edge of the third type of relativity—namely, variations in substance. Such substantive differences in lists of human rights should rarely be accepted. Rights that very in form and interpretation still may be "universal" in an important sense if the substantive list of rights can be said to have considerable international normative universality. There may also be a weaker universality even in the midst of considerable substantive diversity—for example, if there is a large common core with relatively few differences "around the edges." Or if there are strong statistical regularities and the outliers are few, and are clearly overshadowed by the central tendency. I am what some uncomfortable with the degree of relativity implied by even such an extended notion of "universality" but some such variations are perhaps defensible.

Universal Rights

Another important consideration is the extent to which the listed rights are aggregated. At the level of such broad categories as civil, political, economic, and social rights, there is widespread agreement that "universality" is required; any defensible list must include rights from all these categories. As we disaggregate. However, the permissible range of relativity expands, in part because desegregation is largely a process of interpretation, in a broad sense of that term.

Thus we see once more and in greater detail that we do not face an either or choice between cultural relativism and universal human rights. Rather, we need to combine the universality of human rights and their particularity, and thus accept a certain limited relativity for even universal human rights.

Culture and Relativism

The cultural basis of cultural relativism must be considered too, especially because numerous contemporary arguments against universal human rights standards strive for the cause of cultural relativism but actually are entirely without culture basis. Standard arguments for cultural relativism rely on such examples as the pre-colonial African village, Native American tribes, and traditional Islamic social systems, but we have seen that human rights are foreign to such communities, which employed other mechanisms to protect and realize human dignity.

Such communities, however, are increasingly the exception rather than the rule. They are not, for example, the communities of the teeming slums that hold an ever-growing proportion of the population of most third world states. Even most rural areas of the Third World have been substantially penetrated, and the local culture 'corrupted,' by foreign practices and institutions, including the modern state, the money economy, and "western" values, products, and practices. In the Third World today we see most often not the persistence of traditional; culture in the face of modern intrusions, or even the development of syncretism cultures and values, but rather a disruptive "westernization" cultural confusion, or the enthusiastic embrace of "modern" practices and values. In other words, the traditional culture advanced to justify cultural relativism far too often no longer exists. But communitarian defense of traditional practices usually cannot be extended to modern nation states and contemporary nationalist regimes.

Therefore, while recognizing the legitimate claims of self-determination and cultural relativism, we must be alert to cynical manipulation of a dying, lost, or even mythical cultural past. We must not be misled by complaints of the inappropriateness of "Western" human rights made by repressive regimes whose practices have at best only the most tenuous connection to the indigenous culture: communitarian rhetoric too often cloaks the depredations of corrupt and often Westernized or deracinated elites.

Argumentative Cultural

Arguments of cultural relativism are far too often made by economic and political elites that have long since left traditional culture behind. While this may represent a fundamentally admirable effort to retain or recapture cherished traditional values, it is at least ironic to see largely Westernized elites warning against the value and practices they have adopted. At their best, such arguments tend to be dangerously paternalistic. For example "villagization," which was supposed to reflect traditional African conceptions, was accomplished in Tanzania only by force, against the vocal and occasionally even violent opposition of much of the population. And even such a troubling sincerity is unfortunately rare.

Arguments of cultural relativism regularly involve urban elites eloquently praising the glories of village life—a life that they or their parents or grandparents struggled hard to escape and to which they have not the slightest intention of returning. Government officials denounce the corrosive individualism of western values—while they line their pockets with the proceeds of massive corruption, drive imported luxury automobiles, and plan European or American vacations. Leaders sing the praise of traditional communities – while they wield arbitrary power antithetical to traditional values. Purse development politicians that systematically undermine traditional communities, and replace traditional leaders with corrupt cronies and party hacks. Such cynical manipulation of tradition occurs everywhere. Let me cit, however, a few examples from Africa, where "some leaders have even resorted to picking out certain elements of traditional African culture to anesthetize the masses. Despite what is said, this frequently has little to do with a return to the positive, authentic dimensions of African tradition"

Other Views

In Malawi, President Hastings Kamuza Banda utilizes "traditional courts" to deal with political opponents outside the regular legal system. For example – Orton and Vera Chirwa, after being kidnapped from Zambia, were brought before a "traditional court" made up of five judges and three tribal chiefs, all appointed directly by Banda. While there was a prosecutor, no defense attorney was allowed, and the only possible appeal was to Banda personally. Such procedures have not the slightest connection with authentic traditional practices. In Zaire, President Mobutu has created the authentic traditional basis. In fact, it is essentially a revival of the colonial practice of 'curve labour'. In Niger, Samaries, traditional youth organizations have been "revived," but not so much out of a respect for traditional culture as "to replace party organizations so as channel youthful energies away from polities". And Macias Nguema of Equatorial Guinea, probably the most vicious ruler independent black Africa has seen, called himself "Grand Master of Popular Education, Science, and Traditional Culture," a title that might be comical were the situation not so tragic.

The cynicism of many claims of cultural relativism can also be seen in the fact that far too often they are for foreign consumption only. The same elites that raise culture as a defense against external criticisms based on universal human rights often ruthlessly suppress inconvenient local customs whether of the majority or of a minority. National unification certainly will require substantial sacrifices of local customs, but the lack of local cultural sensitivity shown by many national elites that strongly advocate an international cultural relativism suggests a very high degree of self-interest.

Furthermore, a number of regrettably common practices, such as disappearances, arbitrary arrest and detention, or torture, are entirely without cultural basis. Idi Amin, Pol Pot, and death squads of EI Salvador cannot be attributed to local culture; while these names have become justly synonymous with modern barbarism. Such practices are not an expression of established cultural traditions.

In traditional cultures—at least the kinds of traditional cultures that might justify deviations from international human rights standards—people are not victims of the arbitrary decision of rulers whose principal claim to power is their control of modern instrument of force and administration. In traditional cultures, communal customs and practices usually provide each person with a place in society and a certain amount of dignity and protection. Furthermore, there usually are reciprocal bonds between ruler and ruled and between rich and poor. The human rights violations of most Third World regimes are as antithetical to such cultural traditions as they are to "Western" human rights conceptions. In fact, authentic traditional cultural practices and values can be an important check on abuses of arbitrary power. Traditional African cultures, for example, usually were strongly constitutional, with major customary limits on rules; as a Booth Maxim says, "A chief is a chief by the people." Not only are these traditional checks a resource that human rights advocates may be able tap, but it has even been argued that transgressions of traditional limits have figured in the collapse of some recent regimes.

Justification of Cultural

Finally, there are substantive human rights limits on even well-established cultural practices, however difficult it may be to specify and defend particular account of what those practices are. For example—sexual, racial, Ethnic, and religious discriminations have been widely practiced but are indefensible today. Likewise, the depth of the tradition of anti-Semitism in the west is no defense for the maintenance of the practice. This is not to say that certain cultural differences cannot justify even fundamental deviations from "universal" human rights standards, but if cultural relativism is to guarantee local self-determination, rather than clock despotism, we must insist on a strong, authentic cultural basis, as well as on the presence of alternative mechanisms to guarantee basic human dignity, before we justify cultural derogations from universal human rights.

Assessing Claims of Cultural Relativism

The internal normative consensus on human rights presents a strong prima facie case for a relatively strong universalism—that is, for weak cultural relativism. Even if this "consensus" is largely the compliment of vice to virtue, it does reveal widely shared notions of "virtue." An underlaying "universal" moral position that compels at least the appearance of assent from even the cynical and corrupt. Furthermore, as I have argued above, in the conditions of modern society human rights are a particularly appropriate mechanism to protect human dignity. The modern state, the modern economy, and associated "modern" values tend to create communities of relatively autonomous individuals who lack the place and protection provided by traditional society. And regardless of the relative degree of individual autonomy, people today face the particularly threatening modern state and the especially fierce buffeting of the ever-changing modern economy. Rights held equally by all against the state-right, that both limit its legitimate range of action and require positive protection against certain predictable economic, social, and political contingencies—are a seemingly natural and necessary response to typically modern threats to human dignity and basic human values, traditional and modern alike.

Rights are formulate with certain basis violation, or standard threats to human dignity, in mind therefore, the easiest way to overcome the presumption of universality is to demonstrate that the anticipated violation is not standard in that society, that the value is justifiably not considered basis in that society, or that the object of the right is guaranteed by an alternative mechanism. To overcome the presumption of universality, one would have to show that the underlying cultural vision of human nature or society is both morally defensible and incompatible with the implementation of the "universal" human right in question.

Human Rights

Which recognize right to life, liberty, and security of the person; the guarantee of legal personality; and protections against slavery, arbitrary arrest, detention, or exile, and inhuman or degrading treatment. These are so clearly connected to basic cross-cultural requirements of human dignity, and are stated in sufficiently general terms, that any morally defensible contemporary form of social organization must recognize them (although perhaps not necessarily as inalienable rights) I am even tempted to say that conceptions of human nature or society that are incompatible with such rights would be indefensible almost by definition. Such civil rights as freedom of conscience, speech, and association may be a bit more relative. Because they assume the existence and positive evaluation of relatively autonomous individuals, and they may be of questionable applicability in strong, thriving traditional communities. In such communities, however, they would rarely be at issue. If traditional practices truly are based on and protect culturally accepted conceptions of human dignity, then members of such a community simply will not have the desire or need to claim such civil rights. In the more typical contemporary case, however, in which the relatively autonomous individual faces the modern state, they too would seem to be universally demanded; it is hard for me to imagine a defensible modern conception of human dignity that did not include at least most of these rights. A similar argument can be made for the economic and social rights of the Universal Declaration.

The Declaration does list some rights that are best viewed as "interpretation", subject much greater cultural relativity. For example, the right of free and full consent of intending spouses reflects a specific cultural interpretation of marriage that is of relatively recent origin and by no means universal today, even in the west. Notice, however, that the right is subordinate to the right to marry and to found a family, for which there is a strong cross-cultural consensus.

Finally, we should note that even the strongest cultural relativist faces a particularly serious problem where cultures clash or are undergoing substantial transformation, as is the case in much of the Third World. In evaluating customary practices that involve otherwise justifiable deviations from or interpretations of prima facie universal human rights, we often face the problem of "modern" individuals or groups who reject traditional practices. Should we give priority to the idea of community self-determination and permit the enforcement of customary practices against modern "Deviants," even if this violates "universal" human rights? Or should individual self-determination prevail, thus sanctioning claims of universal human rights against traditional society? We return to this issue in chapter 8, but a few brief comments are in order here.

Recent Trends in Women's Rights

In a recent discussion of women's rights in Africa, Rhoda Howard suggests an attractive and widely applicable compromise strategy on a combination of practical and moral grounds. Howard argues against an outright ban on such practices as child betrothal and widow inheritance, but she also argues strongly for national legislation that permits women (and the families of female children) to "opt out" of traditional practices. Where practical, guaranteeing a right to "opt out" of traditional practices in favour of "universal" human rights or alternative human rights interpretations seems ideal, for it permits an individual in effect to choose his or her culture, or the terms on which he or she will participate in the traditional culture.

Conclusion

Conflicting practices, however, may sometimes be irreconcilable for example, a right to private ownership of the means of production is incompatible with the maintenances of a village society in which families hold only right of use to communally owned land; allowing individuals to opt out and fully own their land would destroy the traditional system. Less dramatic, full freedom of religion, including a right to apostasy is incompatible with certain well-established traditional Islamic views. But even such conflict may sometimes be resolved, or at least minimized, by the physical or legal separation of adherents of old and new values. Although separation may be difficult-given the interpenetration of rural and urban sectors, for example—it may be possible, particularly with practices that are not material to the maintenance or essential integrity of either culture.

Nevertheless, a choice must sometimes be made, at least by default, between competing practices or conceptions of human rights. Such cases take us out of the realm in which useful general guidelines are possible. Fortunately though, they are the exception rather than the rule. I believe that we can justifiably insist on some form of weak cultural relativism—that is, a fairly strong universalism. It may be necessary to allow limited cultural variations in the form and interpretation of particular human rights, but we must insist on their fundamental moral universality. Human rights are, to use an appropriately paradoxical phrase, relatively universal.

Human Rights Education in Unpeace Building

Form Theory to Practice

United Nations "Peace-building" operations offer new and promising opportunities to develop and apply a general approach to human rights education. An example of this potential is the education, information, and training programme of the Human Rights Component of the United Nations Transitional Authority in Cambodia (UNTAC). The peace plan, under which the United Nations went to Combodia in 1992-93, provided a broad mandate that called for a concentrated and intense effort to carry out human rights education at all levels and of all types. The experience is instructive not only for other possible peace operations under UN auspices, but also as a test case for conceiving a strategy for human rights education and carrying in out under severe time constraints. It is thus a case of a comprehensive approach toward human rights education in both theory and practice.

A new direction of operational support for human rights education emerged with the Security Council's decisions to implement comprehensive political settlement to regional conflicts and its recognition that human rights could provide the normative framework for institutional modifications and constitutional reform, as well as self-determination through free and fair elections. There are three recent examples where education about human rights was given an explicit place in the mandates of UN operations, namely, those in EI Salvador, Cambodia, and Haiti. This is a new dimension on UN peace-keeping since human rights was absent from peace-keeping as traditionally practiced before the late 1980s. Peace-keeping operations did not include either monitoring human rights or informing populations about these rights. With the end of the cold war and the greatly enhanced expectations placed on the United Nations, unfettered by the veto that had blocked so many possible responses to complex emergencies, the Security Council referred more and more frequently to human rights.

The framework for UN peace operation is set out in An Agenda for peace, produced in response to the historic summit of heads of state and government on January 31, 1992. The report defines and reviews the tree traditional areas of preventive diplomacy. Peace-making, and peace-keeping, plus a fourth, called "Post-conflict peace-building." Whereas preventive diplomacy seeks to avoid the outbreak of a violent conflict, peace-building seeks to prevent its recurrence. Designed for situations like EI Salvador and Cambodia, where warring parties agree to end hostilities and work toward reconciliation and rehabilitation, but remain suspicious of each other and politically ambitious, peace-building should include, in the words of the Secretary General, "disarming the previously warring parties and the restoration of order, the custody and possible destruction of weapons, repatriating refugees, advisory and training support for security personnel, monitoring elections, advancing efforts to protect human rights, reforming or strengthening governmental institution and promoting formal and informal process of political participation"? This function also can entails "Support for the transformation of deficient national structures and capabilities and for the strengthening of new democratic institution," in shout "the construction of new environment", "Human rights education within the framework of peace-building has been tested in several major UN operations, especially in UNTAC. This chapter examines the application of peace-building through human rights education as practices by the United Nations in Cambodia and suggests some general guidelines for human rights educations part of peace-building.

UNTAC was an experiment in implementing a broad mandate to reach all levels of society during a brief period. The official duration of the transitional period was just under two years, but the effective period for implementing this mandate was approximately one year. It was an impossibly short period to transform a society, yet a degree of democratic empowerment of occurred and is continuing to affect the political process in Cambodia. To review this experience, I begin with the mandate, that is, what the parties and the UN Security Council asked UNTAC to do, and then discuss how, on the basis of that mandate, a strategy for a countrywide human rights education programme was implemented. With this mandate and strategy in mind, I make some general observations about the opportunities and obstacles facing internationally managed human rights education through the formal and informal structures.

UNTAC's Human Rights Education Mandate and Strategy

The mandate of UNTAC's human rights education programme is set out in the Paris Peace Agreement of October 1991 and Report of the secretary general of February 1992. The secretary general's report to the Security Council on Cambodia says that "The development and dissemination of a human rights education programme is foreseen as the cornerstone of UNTAC's activities in fostering respect for human rights." This statement is based on UNTAC's responsibility as set out in Article 16 of the Paris Agreement for "fostering an environment in which human rights shall be ensured" and section E of Annex I, which says that UNTAC shall make provision for "development and implementation of a programme of human rights education to promote respect for and understating of human rights." The meaning of "education" is broad; it implies "teaching" in formal and informal learning environments, as well as "training" and "information". With respect to formal teaching, the secretary general's report envisaged "that UNTAC would also work closely with existing educational administrative structures in Cambodia to ensure that human rights education is appropriately included in the curriculum at all levels. Including children, adults and special groups" (para 13) significantly the report states that Cambodians must fully understand both the content and the significance of those rights and freedoms in order to be in a position to know when and how to protect them properly. This is especially important in an environment in which the framing of a new Cambodian Constitution containing human rights guarantees will be on the national agenda.... Such a civic education programme would be developed in a manner that is culturally sensitive and generally "accessible" to Cambodians, its dissemination would reply upon all channels of communication available in the country. Included printed materials (words and pictures) cultural events and presentations, radio and television media, videocassette distribution mobile teaching units, etc., (para 12-13)

"Training" is also used in the human rights section of the secretary-general's report in four places:" Complementary training" to civic education (para.14); "some training" in the application of guidelines and materials targeted to civil servants (para.16); "supplementary training" for law enforcement officials and the judiciary, "especially in the areas of fundamental criminal procedure" (para.17) and "Training" of UNTAC personnel in the area of law enforcement and judicial functions (*ibid*). The term "training" is intended in these passages in the proper sense of imparting skills necessary for the performance of certain specialized tasks.

Thus while the secretary general's report does not make the distinction between types and levels of education. It does providing guidance on training and information and target groups for these educational activities. The implementation of these broad guidelines required a more specific strategy and plan of action.

After determining that the mandate included all levels and types of education, the Human Rights Component devised and implemented a six-step strategy. Step one was to identify the target groups to whom educational activities would be directed, on the basis of studies of Cambodian Society made by specialized agencies and programmes (such as United Nations Educational, Scientific and Cultural Organisation (UNESCO], the United Nations Children's Fund [UNICEF], and the United Nations Development programme [UNDP]), consultations with international NGOs, with experience in Cambodia, and Cambodian staff members and indigenous NGOs. The fifteen groups thus targeted included two from UNTAC (UNTAC Civil Police and electoral staff). Seven from the existing administrative structures (Police, teachers, university students, ministerial official, other civil servants, political party representatives, judges and prosecutors); and six from the civil society (defenders, human rights associations, women's associations, journalists, monks, and health professionals).

Notably absent from the target groups within the civil society were trade unions. The reasons were that, as confirmed by consultations with the International Labour Organisation and the Asian American Free Labour Association, the labour movement was neither independent nor sufficiently organized to provide a context for learning activities. The military, both UN forces and those of the existing administrative structures, was initially included. The Cambodian troops were to be cantoned in special sites where course would be organized. However, the failure to implement the demobilization and cantonment phase of the peace plan excluded this possibility. Nevertheless, in cooperation with the dissemination unit of the local delegation of the

International Committee of the Red Cross, several provincial human rights officers setup ad hoc training for the military.

The second element of this strategic planning was a determined the specific expectations with respect to each group and in light of the secretary general's report. In most cases, the main goal was a basic understanding of the concepts of human rights, the content of the international standards, their applicability to Cambodia, and their relations to the lives and work of the learners.

The third step was to assemble the necessary human and financial resources beyond the initial staff of four in the Education, Training, and Information Unit in Phnom Penh (a training officer, an information officer, an NGO relations officer, and a unit chief). Eventually the Phnom Penh staff assigned to the Education, Training and Information Unit was increased by five (two police trainers, one education, officer in charge of women's projects, a training officer to head the mobile teams, and a senior advisor for media projects). Eventually aided by four training assistance and two UN volunteers. A major staffing addition, not foreseen in the secretary general's report was the appointment in late 1992 of twenty one provincial human rights officers, whose responsibilities included education, training, and information, and twenty one training assistants Khmer speaking educators, trained by the Component and assigned to each provincial human rights officer, working full time on training at the provincial level. Such staffing is reality small compared with other components of the mission, but is significant compared to what is normally available for human rights education.

To supplement the financial resources UNTAC launched an appeal to governments in October 1992, which resulted in a Trust Fund for a Human rights Education programme in Cambodia, with about $1.8 million eventually expended to contract services among local and international NGOs having specialized staff and experience to target groups that component staff were unable to train directly.

The fourth and fifth steps consisted in setting a timetable for each of the projects and implementing them. There was a sense of urgency to proceed with the implementation because of the extremely short time available to the mission, and the conviction that such resources and political will were not likely to be found again. Moreover, bureaucratic delays to obtain approvals from administrative and financial services in Phnom Penh and New York shortened even more the effective time for project implementation.

The sixth and final step was project evaluation, which varied from one project to the next and often took the minimal form of questionnaires completed by participants or a self-evaluation session. Evaluation was more systematic with the police training, law school, health professionals, teacher training colleges, and women's groups. In general, the degree of assimilation of concepts and skill appears directly proportional to the links established between the content of teaching and the daily lives of the learners. Statistic was maintained of the various training activities, although this should be done more systematically in future operations and outside evaluator should be employed. This six-step strategy was implemented in both formal and informal education.

Formal Education

When UNTAC arrived, education in Cambodia was at a virtual standstill, 75 per cent of the teachers, about 67 per cent of primary and secondary level students, and almost 80 per cent of higher education students having been eliminated or fled the country. Formal education facilities had all been closed down or put to other use. It was in this context that UNTAC sought to develop teaching and training on human rights in the schools and universities. Using a slightly different approach for each.

Even where formal education is grossly deficient, the development of human rights education requires working through existing structures. Thus UNTAC obtained from

Ministry of Education a decree making human rights part of the official curriculum of civic education in the primary and Lower secondary schools and instructing the provincial education directors to cooperate with provincial human rights officers in setting up programmes in the schools. UNTAC printed teaching materials, conducted briefings and courses for teachers in the schools and in the teacher training colleges, sent mobile teams to the various provinces to give courses of one to two weeks to various group, and supported several projects directed at primary and secondary education through the Trust Fund.

The university audience was highly receptive to human rights teaching? UNTAC's human rights education efforts focused primarily on law and medical students. At the country's only law school. UNTAC prepared and taught a four-hour a week course for a three month period for some 242 students, culminating in an examination. Student motivation and learning curve were both remarkably high in spite of their low level of preparation. Students were particularly receptive to teaching methods that employed critical thinking (not typical in the university) that they could apply to other subjects in law school, rather than the exegesis of abstract international texts. To succeed this method has to place the academic value of free inquiry ahead of the diplomatic propensity to avoid controversial political issues. Teaching, even through the United Nations has little impact if it is based on cautiously worded official positions. It requires a willingness to link human rights concepts to real-life situations. By taking on an issue on which passions run high in Cambodia (such as the presence of ethnic Vietnamese), students were trained in a four step mode of analysis: (1) Establish the facts impartially and thoroughly; (2) identify the human rights issues involved; (3) analyze each human rights issue in light of the fact situation; and (4) make appropriate policy recommendations. The most difficult step was the first, since Cambodian students have very little experience with critically assessing sources of information, in part because impartial and reliable information is scarce and in part because "facts" are often created to fit preconceived conclusions. Dr. Allen Keller and his colleagues had similar experiences as the Medical Faculty and the college of Nursing during the projects.

Informal Education

The strategy for "informal education had to be tailored to meet the need and circumstances of each of the target groups. Part of the training, especially in the first months of mission, was directed at UNTAC itself, through briefings for civil police and district electoral supervisors. However, the component's main human rights education effort was directed toward the Cambodian population. In particular, efforts were made through training to reach the key categories of the emerging civil society and public officials and through the media to reach all segments of the population.

The mandate state that "UNTAC would also work closely with... special groups, [including] those individuals best placed to be further disseminators of information such as teachers and community leaders". This section of the mandate was interpreted to mean that human rights education should be directed toward democratic empowerment of the emerging civil society and public officials. The principal forces of civil society in Cambodia are the Buddhist clergy, the free press, and NGOs, mainly those focusing on human rights, women and development.

The Buddhist clergy constitute a particularly effective vehicle for reaching the public at large, especially in remote areas. Buddhism and the monks were severely victimized during the Khmer Rouge period. According to a leading authority on the period, "Khmer Rouge policy toward Buddhism constituted one of the most brutal and through going attacks on religion in modern history". The population of monks was reduced from about sixty thousand to less than one thousand. The Vietnamese installed government in Phnom Penh tolerated the monks, although the National Front for Construction and Defense, an organ of the party, supervised them closely. After arrival of the United Nations, Buddhism flourished and several monks who returned from exile became leaders in the human rights movement. For example, the venerable Mahan Ghosannda, the Supreme Patriarch and Co-founder of the Inter Religious Mission for peace in Cambodia, is an inspirational figure among NGOs. He and his fellow monks found full compatibility between the teachings of the Buddha and international human rights, the following meditation typifies his view that human rights are universal.

During his lifetime, the Buddha lobbied for peace and human rights. We can learn much from a lobbyist like him. Human rights begin when each man becomes a brother and each woman becomes a sister, when we honestly care for each other. Then Cambodians will help Jews, and Jews will help Africans, and Africans will help others. We will all become servants for each other's rights..... Any real peace will not favour East, West, North or South. A peaceful Cambodia will be friendly to all. Peace is nonviolent, and so we Cambodians will remain nonviolent toward all as we rebuild our country. Peace is based on justice and freedom, and so a peaceful Cambodia will be just and free.

Through marches, teaching, lobbying with governmental and parliamentary leaders and spiritual guidance to the populations, which is 90-95 per cent Buddhist, the clergy has popularized constitutionalism and human rights, even in remote areas. During the first year of UNTAC, the Phnom Penh authorities resisted the Component's attempts to set up systematic training for this category. The active participation of monks in the human rights associations, including regularly providing meeting and office space in the WATS (Pagodas), nonetheless allowed the Component to work with them in human rights education. In early 1993 it became possible to implement a more systematic strategy through a Trust Fund project that trained "master trainers" who in turn prepared hundred of monks to teach human rights to their congregations.

The experience with the monks has implications for human rights education in other peace-building contexts. With the exception of societies where organized religion is subservient to repressive government, the main religions provide both a source of understanding of prevailing values and a cultural context which must be integrated into teaching. Religions are thus a vehicle for reaching widely and deeply into society. It is unfortunate that this book does not contain a chapter illustrate its importance. No doubt certain intolerant interpretations of major religions and practices of most religions are problematic for human rights, but there is support for the claim that "Faith in human rights education through religious beliefs enormous.

Journalists were already receiving through a UNESCO programme, funded by the Danish government, as well as though the University of Phnom Penh under an arrangement with the French government. The component integrated human rights teaching significantly into these programmes. The UNESCO programme was primarily aimed at skills development for the journalists from all three factions and representing both prints and broadcast journalism. The most common substantive theme of their sessions was human rights, including issues of freedom of expression and human rights aspects of current events in Cambodia. Freedom of expression was generally respected during the transitional period, and there was hope that it would continue to thrive under the new constitution of September 23, 1993 which guarantees freedom to express opinions and to publish (Article 41), some twenty newspapers are published in Khmer, English, French, and Chinese some of which criticize the government and its leader freely. Subsequently developments relating to a new press law, the closing of newspapers, and the murder of a journalist have placed these accomplishments in jeopardy.

Nevertheless, the international and domestic preoccupation with such incidents is a sign that serious debate over freedom of the press is taking place.

The Cambodian experience illustrates two dimensions of the relation between human rights education and journalism that are more generally, relevant. First regarding the status and freedoms of journalists, it is essential that human rights education activities that reach journalists, civil servants, the police, politicians and NGOs focus attention of the distinction between protected and prohibited speech, and on the rights and responsibilities of journalists. In this field the accusation of imposing Western values should be matter of open discussion rather than an inhibiting factor. Examples abound to illustrate how in non western societies, a free press can be the rampart of the civil society against authoritarian rule and a critical element of democratic empowerment.

The second dimension of the relations between human rights education and journalism is that journalists themselves have much to learn about how to report a human rights story. UNESCO had it right in Cambodia by brining human rights concepts into skills training. The persistent lack of professional ethics and skills among Cambodia journalists demonstrates the need to sustain this effort well beyond the short duration of the peace mission. A comprehensive human rights education programme should not tell journalists to preach human rights but rather equip them to identify the rights and remedies relevant to a story. It should always be remembered that these issues are literally matters of life and death in most countries where peace-building takes place.

According to the secretary general's report, "UNTAC would also expect to collaborate with non-governmental organisation (NGOs) operating in Cambodia for this purpose as well as to encourage the establishment of indigenous human rights associations". The proliferation of NGOs independent of the state and party structures, was described by the special representative of the secretary general on human rights in

Cambodia as the "first step towards a civil society in Cambodia after its destruction between 1975 and 1975". During the transitional period, UNTAC handled the registration of associations and was quite liberal in accepting applications. Indigenous human rights association and women's organisation were both partners and learners in the component's human rights education effort.

Five human rights groups were functioning in Cambodia during the transitional period, with combined membership claimed to be in the hundreds of thousands. The component focused its efforts on capacity building so that these groups could become effective advocates and defendants of human rights. Members of these associations were trained as human rights educators, defenders, and monitors. They were provided with materials to conduct their own educational work and participated in component sponsored conferences. Seminars and discussion groups where they could refine their policies and strategies. The key organisations were allotted substantial grants from the UN Trust Fund to organize their own education and training programme and to send delegation to the UN Commission on Human Rights and the Bangkok preparatory conference for the World conference on Human rights. A major objective of this support was to mobilize international and regional NGOs to work with their Cambodian counterparts. One of the trust fund projects, the Human rights task force for the Cambodian Elections, was under the responsibility of one U.S., based and six Asian based Human rights groups. The Task Force prepared human rights activists from each of the main indigenous human rights associations to monitor human rights during the election. As a result these associations provided by far the largest numbers of elation observers registered by the Electoral Component. The Task Force facilitated planning and coordination of activities of these groups and was so successful at this effort that it was continued after the elections as the Cambodian Human rights Task Force with additional funding from the Trust Fund.

Women's NGOs were also active partners in Human rights education. Women constitute more than 60 per cent of the Cambodian population as a result of mass murder and civil war. The lack of equal educational and employment opportunities had deep cultural roots, which required special efforts in human rights education. Courses were run by the component in Phnom Penh and in the provinces, providing both basic educations (introduction to concepts) are in depth "training of trainers" for these associations. They were also provided with trust fund grants to conduct their own human rights education activates or to work with international NGOs. For example an innovative project was conducted with support from the Trust Fund by the Decade of Human Rights Education. (This programme is described in the Chapter by Donna Hicks in this Book.)

After UNTAC's departure, human rights associates continued to be a vital part of Cambodian social and political life. Seven more human rights NGOs have emerged. UNTAC had supported the creation of a coalition of fourteen human rights, women's, and development NGOs, called Ponleu Khmer, which was particularly active during the drafting of the constitution. Ponleu Khmer continued after the proclamation of the constitution and the departure of UNTAC to educate the population about participatory democracy and to push for a sense of accountability on the part of elected officials and civil servants. In June 1994, nine human rights NGOs founded the Cambodian Human Rights Coordination Committee in order to strengthen links and improve exchanges of information. In 1994 the Cambodian Institute of Human Rights Finalized and obtained official approval of the new human rights curriculum for grades 1 to 11 and organized four month long constitutional workshops for professors at the law school, government leaders, members of the Assembly, persons trained in law and judges, in an effort to help them better understand the constitution and take it more seriously.

Specific references was also made in the secretary general's report to officials of existing administrative structures, and in particular police, judges, prosecutors, and civil servants. The Component's strategy was to make officials aware of the obligations the parties had accepted in the peace process and their specific responsibilities as public servants. The second objective was to prepare them for a more responsible and accountable public service under the government to be created following the adoption of the constitution. The strategy was implemented by provincial and Phnom Penh staff of the Component rather than through the Trust Fund. Two police trainers were added to the staff, as was one person experienced in working with civil servants.

With respect to judges and prosecutors, the Component worked with UNTAC's Civil Administration Component on joint training activities following the adoption, in September 1992, of the Provisions Relating to the Judiciary and Criminal Law and procedure Applicable in Cambodia during the Transitional Period (Transitional Provisions). Component staff took part as instructors in courses held for the judges and prosecutors and developed a special series of judicial training activities. In July 1993 a three-week, all-day programme on the judicial functions and independence of the judiciary was organized by the Centre for the independence of judges who had been or were likely to be appointed to the Court of Appeals and the Supreme Court.

Complementing the training of judges was the preparation of persons to represent the accused in court. The near total elimination of all lawyers during the 1975-78 period and thirteen years of one-party rule from 1979-1992 left Cambodia without anything resembling a bar association. No private attorneys or public defenders and practiced in the country in any capacity since 1975. The transitional Provisions guaranteed the right to legal assistance for any persons accused of a crime or a misdemeanor. Because of the dearth of attorneys, the Traditional Provisions stipulated that anyone with a secondary school diploma, or a family member of the accused, regardless of level of education, may represent the accused in court. In order to provide a minimal level or competency for these potential "defenders", the Defenders Training Programme was created, which has continued as a project of the International Human Rights Law Group.

Civil Servants participated in the two-week, courses run by the mobile teams. Many were employed by the local administration without being party members and, in fact, were sympathetic to indigenous human rights NGOs, although they did not reveal this fact to their employers. Separate and special course were developed for the Police, who were surprisingly receptive to the training, Interactive and student centered teaching methods worked well with his group. Of course police training can only have an impact when conducted over the long-term where there is the political will and the institution infrastructure to sustain a professional police accountable to elected representatives.

The experience of human rights education for public officials in Cambodia suggests three considerations of more general relevance. The first is that local authorities are likely to accept training of their officials only if it is handled by international officials. Trainers should be UN staff, even if on temporary status. Second, civil servants relate human rights to their professional work when there is an official code of professional conduct. Of course, the UN Code of conduct for law Enforcement Officials is the appropriate reference for police training. Other codes should be used for other categories of public officials, such as the basic principles on the Independence of the judiciary and similar texts for prosecutors and the legal profession. Their especially in societies that have undergone years of civil war and political repression, human rights education during the presence of a UN mission can only be the first step in a much longer process of systematic training. Therefore, human rights education should seek, during the mission, support for the planning and financing of training institutes in particular a judicial training institute and a civilian police academy.

A common feature of human rights training in both the civil society and among public officials was a hunger for knowledge about human rights. Past experience with violent conflict and a genuine conviction that the peace-building will bring about a more just society undoubtedly contributed to the ready acceptance of major human rights education initiatives by local officials. These conditions, which are likely to exist in other peace-building operations, suggest that those in charge of implementing human rights education should act rapidly and develop ambitious projects that take full advantage of the opening provided by the existing administrative structures.

In developing a strategy for human rights information, the component's task was to develop a culturally relevant human rights information, the Component's task was media. Cultural relevance meant that the message to be disseminated would be consonant with concepts and principles of Cambodian society today. These concepts and principles were found in the Buddhist religion, which provides a spiritual basis for human rights action. The component, in close Collaboration with the TV and Graphic Design units of UNTAC's Information and Education Divisions, developed a human rights information campaign on two pillars, printed materials and audiovisual media.

As regards Print media, Khmer artists were used to develop a logo representing a Cambodian landscape with the sunlight of human rights illuminating all aspects of Cambodian life in peace. It was used on T-Shirts, Posters, and book covers, such as the cover of a special Khmer edition of the Universal Declaration of Human Rights.

The production and distribution of printed material served there purposes. Several items were used for teaching, such as the four hundred thousand training leaf lets. The compilation of Khmer translations of official UN texts, a found hundred page book of which 100,000 copies were distributed, served as legal reference for NGOs, defenders, and public officials. Most of the material were aimed at creating a positive including 500,000 basic leaflets 200,000 stickers, 100,000 copies of the Universal Declaration 100,000 balloons and 82,000 posters, specifically the message of these materials was that peace in Cambodia must be built on respect for human rights.

The strategy for Broadcast media covered both television and radios, which are particularly important in High of the low level of education and literacy in Cambodia. The human rights "message" was simplified as such as possible and made attractive by using symbols, stories and popular actors. The dissemination of audiovisual materials was done through all existing channels. Video and audiocassettes were offered to all Cambodian broadcast authorities as well as those outside Cambodia with Khmer programmes directed at Cambodia. In addition, five hundred cassettes with a human rights video were distributed through district electoral supervisors, provincial human rights officers, and indigenous human rights groups, feedback from these circles in dictates that frequent showings were organized even in the remotest areas. UNTAC's radio and television production units ran into numerous delays but eventually had considerable reach. Radio UNTAC, for example, began in October 1992, producing only one thirty minute programme of "news" (*i.e.* excerpts from the UN spokesman's daily briefing), but by election time in May 1993 managed to broadcast fifteen hours a day for seven days a week". Remote areas were reached by twice-daily transmission from voice of America from Bangkok and by distribution by the electoral component in the provinces of a hundred copies of each Ratio UNTAC Programme.

The presence of a peace-building mission generates high expectations among the general population, virtually guaranteeing enthusiastic participation in special events organized them. International Human rights Day offers an ideal opportunity for massive public participations, as was the case on December 10, 1992 when the Component, organized celebration throughout Cambodia, with songs, drama productions, speeches by human rights organizations, and distribution of Khmer-language banners, stickers, posters, leaflets, and the brochure containing the Universal Declaration. A poster contest was organized for children under fifteen on "what human rights means to me "resulting in ten thousand posters, the best of which were published, along with selected texts in English and Khmer on Children's rights, in a book called A Dream of Peace. The role of culture is essential to transmission of knowledge and understanding, and traditional means of cultural expression should be a part of a human rights education strategy. UNTAC, with UNESO, produced a series of traditional musical performances, comic books, and series of posters.

The impact of informal training activities and of the mass distribution of printed materials and of television, video, and radio productions has not been tested scientifically. UNTAC estimated that approximately 120,000 people directly benefited from education and training and that the figure for mass communication, considering the population of more than 9 million, the wide availability of radios, the area covered by transmission, and the dissemination of cassettes of the programmes, is probably several million. There are many signs that the basic message that people in Cambodia have certain rights that must be respected by all has penetrated. One year after UNTAC's departure, observes in Cambodia note that the concept and the primacy of human rights have become part of the public discourse in Cambodia to a degree previously unknown.

Conclusions Lessons Learned

The lessons of approximately one year of implementing a programme of Human rights education, training, and information in Cambodia are relevant more generally to human rights education as a component of peace building. These lessons concern primarily (*a*) the definition of target groups; (*b*) the relationship between human rights as taught and practical realities of daily life; (*c*) relations with the exiting adminis-trative structures; (*d*) methods of teaching; (*e*) administration of extra budgetary funds for educational projects; and (*f*) long term impact of education and training.

The strategy described above proved to be successful insofar as the principal elements of Cambodian society were identified and constituted the major transmitters of knowledge and understanding. What is important to consider in developing strategies for other contexts is to persevere whenever to key target groups has been identified but programme actions have been difficult to implement. For example—it was not until fairly late in the mandate of UNTAC that the Component found appropriate implementing agencies to bring human rights education to health professionals and the Buddhist clergy on a significant scale. Had this not been done, there would have been major gaps in the programme.

Teaching, especially at the beginning of UNTAC's human rights programme, tended to describe the relevance of Buddhist principles and then explain the content of the Universal Declaration and the International Covenants. Student's questions led the instructors to realize that effective education must be linked to the lives of the learners. Moreover, the brevity of the courses meant that this newly acquired knowledge had title chance of being consolidated and transformed into appropriate actions to protect and exercise those rights. Real case studies of violations, for example, have a greater impact than abstract examples. The Women's training Project, in which training was based on Women using drawings and drama to bring out aspects of their daily lives, was the prototype of this approach. The defender's course is another example of an educational activity that is effective when the students are exposed to real courtroom situations.

The local authorities manifested a general willingness not to interfere with practically prepared for such openness, and similar operations should be prepared to move massively into intensive, educational activity. In practice, the opportunities were limited by the availability of staff and funds. Had these two matters been resolved earlier, greater advantage could have been taken of this openness?

There is no doubt that this components programme and other similar ones conducted by the Cambodian Human rights associations were successful in that they introduced large number of people for the first time to basic human rights concepts. Support for these groups and retraining of their trainers are essential to the long-term effectiveness of their efforts. The use of mobile teams is an effective mechanism for mass education at a basic level, but they did not have a systematic inbuilt mechanism for ensuring that the critical follow-up work with course participants would be carried on. Video should be used more frequently, especially in villages, where literacy is low. The most important lesson regarding teaching, methods is that, even in a society like Cambodia where people, especially women, are not generally demonstrative, interactive methods work best. This requires more preparation by the teachers but the results are worth it.

The availability of resources through the Trust Fund was a vital element in the effectiveness of the programme. It would have been considerably more effective if funds had been available sooner and if the administrative procedure were not as heavy as they were. The availability of such a fund at the beginning would have made a considerable difference.

Finally human rights education, like all other aspects of peace-building, is primarily a means of laying long-term foundations for humane governance. The concept of democratic empowerment is helpful as a criterion for conceiving and implementing human rights education projects. This concept is based on a concern for the degree to which the beneficiaries of the project acquire knowledge and skills they can use to participate effectively in decisions affecting their lives. Democratic empowerment of the new government requires assistance in the preparation of key legislation and development and strengthening of national institution. This has been the direction of the successors to the Component, the Phnom Penh office of the UN Centre of Human Rights. In sum, human rights education was tested as part of United Nations pears building in Cambodia on a scale that was unprecedented. Many of the lessons of that experience can be applied elsewhere, if the political will exists to make use of the methods developed by UNTAC in Cambodia and to adapt approaches identified elsewhere in this book to the harsh realities of societies in transition from civil war and political repression to democracy and the rule of law.

REFERENCES

1. See Philip Alston "The Security Council and Human Rights; Lessons to Be learned from the Iraq-Kuwait Crisis and Its Aftermath," Australian year Book of International Law 13(1992); 107-76.
2. UN General Assembly, Report of the Secretary—General on the Work of the Organization, An Agenda for Peace; Preventive Diplomacy, Peace-making and Peace-keeping. Un Doc A/47/ 277/S/24111 (June 17, 1992).32.
3. *Ibid.*, 33-34.
4. According to the Paris Agreement on a Comprehensive Political Settlement of the Cambodia Conflict, the Transitional Period extended from the signing of the Agreement (October 23, 1991) to the transfer of authority from the Constituent Assembly to the new Government (September 24, 1993).
5. Report of the Secretary-General on Cambodia, UN Doc. S/23613 Para 12m This Document is the Principal Source, after the text of the Paris Agreements, of UNTAC's mandate.
6. UNESCO, Inter-Sectoral Basic Needs Assessment Mission to Cambodia 15 January-8, February 1991, Report, Bangkok (February 1991) 10.

7. Part of the explanation for the intense interest of university students in Human Rights is the brutal repression of student demonstrations in 1991, shortly before the arrival of UNTAC.
8. Sometimes, a distinction is made between "informal" and "nonformula" education. For simplicity, I use "informal" for all types of learning that takes place outside the official schools and universities.
9. Report of the Secretary-General, S/23613, Para 13.
10. David Hawk, *"The Photographic Record"*, in Cambodia 1975-1978. Rendervous with Death, ed.Karl D. Jackson (Princeton: Princeton University Press, 1989), 212.
11. *Ibid.*
12. Eva Mysliwiec, *Punishing the Poor, The International Isolation of Kampuchea* (Oxford: Oxfam, 1988). 47.
13. Maha Ghosananda, Step by Step (Berkeley, Calif.: Parallax Press.1992), 70-71.
14. Robert Traer, Faith in Human Rights; Support in Religious Taditions for a Global struggle (Wasington, D.C., Georgetown University, Press, 1991), 219.
15. Report of the Special Representative of the Secretary – General, Mr. Michael Kirby (Australia), on the Situation of Human Rights in Cambodia, submitted in Accordance with Commission resolution 1993/6, UN Doc. E/CN.4 / 1994/73 (February 24,1994) para 159 p. 41.
16. See Bala Chandran, "Cambodia –Media: Free Press Blurs as Editor Goes to Jail", Inter Press Service, July 27, 1994, P.15.
17. Report of the Secretary General S/23613 para 13.
18. Report of the Social Representative para 165, p. 42.
19. Report of the Secretary—General para 6.
20. Zhou mei, Radio UNTAC of Cambodia, Winning Ears, Hearts and Minds (Bangkok, white lots, 1994) 28.
21. Report of the Secretary General, Situation of Human Rights in Cambodia, UN Doc. A/49/635/Add.1 (November 3, 1994), Paras 10-33, pp. 4-10.

Human Rights and Cultural Values

Caste in India

One-seventh of the world's people are Indian. India's population is larger than that of United States and Western Europe, or Latin America and Africa, combined, and the diversity of the Indian people is perhaps even more striking than their numbers. India is the birthplace of two major world religions (Hinduism and Buddhism) has more Muslims than any country in the Middle East of North Africa, and has many other religions of local or regional importance (*e.g.*, Sikhs in the Punjab). Differences between city and countryside (where almost three-fourths of all Indian still live) are striking, and a relatively prosperous modern industrial economy sits loosely and uncomfortably on a largely traditional agricultural economy. Furthermore, this contemporary diversity is matched by a long complex, rich and varied history, as invader, from the Aryans to the British, periodically injected major new elements into and then was gradually absorbed by an increasingly complex culture.

To talk of "India," therefore, requires reducing this complex diversity to manageable proportions, typically by selecting a single place or a single part to stand, however imperfectly, for the whole, I follow the second course, taking Hinduism as the locus of traditional Indian values.

1. 'Human rights' and traditional Indian society: The dominant tendency in the literature is to argue that human rights ideas have been present is all society at all times, but India is a partial exception to this tendency.

But a surprising number of authors argue that human right ideas are present in traditional Indian (Hindu) ideas and practice. Yougindra Khushalani claims that "Hindu civilization had a well-developed system which guaranteed both civil and political as well as the economic, social and cultural rights of the human being"

Taking it for granted that there is a Hindu concept of human rights. And S.K. Sajsena, although not explicitly using the language of human rights, speaks of "Hinduism, with its basic principle of equality of opportunity" and argues that prefeudal Indian society was based on "standards of equality and of the freedom of the individual as an individual". (1967:367,360-61)

In fact, though, social structures and the underlaying social visions of human dignity in traditional India, as in other traditional societies, rest not on human rights but on social duties and status hierarchies: "Indians...base their social structure on duties and obligation rather than on rights." Persons are seen first and by nature as bearers of duties, not right, and whatever rights one does have rest on the discharge of duties or one'status and in traditional Indian (Hindu) society, "people's duties and rights are specified not in terms of their humanity but in terms of specific caste, age and Sex" (Mitra 1982:79), while the caste system made the ascriptive hierarchy so rigid that for all intents and purposes one's duties and rights were almost completely defined by birth.

2. Caste, status and purity: Caste may be defined as a small and named group of persons characterized by endogamy, hereditary membership, and a specific style of life which sometimes includes the pursuit by tradition of a particular occupation and is usually associated with a more or less distinct ritual status in a hierarchical system. (Beteille 1965:46)

The caste system divides the whole society into a large number of hereditary groups, distinguished from one another and connected by three characteristics separation in matters of marriage and contact, whether direct or indirect (food); division of labour, each group having, in theory or by tradition, a profession from which their members can depart only within certain limits; and finally hierarchy, which ranks the groups as relatively superior or inferior to one another. (Dumont 1980:46)

Individual elements of the caste system are common elsewhere: all societies have social hierarchies, with a tendency of different group to separate from one another, and hereditary occupational specialization has usually been the norm, even in the west until very recently. But the combination of these three of separation, division, and hierarchy in the intensity characteristic of India makes the caste system largely unique to south Asia and the division of society into an extremely large number of endogamous groups kept separate by extraordinarily powerful and detailed rules of ritual purity is particularly characteristic of Hindu India.

The most ancient Indian formulas recognizes four castes, or varnas (colours): Brahman, Kshatriya, Vaishya, and Shudra (symbolized by the colours white, red, yellow, and black), which roughly correspond to priests, warriors/rulers, the landed and mercantile classes, and the servcle classes. Below these four varnas were Candelas, "untouchables." It is unclear whether this fourfold (or rather fivefold) division ever accurately desired Indian society.4 but by the third or fourth century A.D. a much more compels system of caste segmentation existed, based on the jati, an endogamous decent group traditionally linked to a particular occupation. Today "there are so many (castes) that is virtually impossible to determine their exact number," the boundaries between castes are maintained by exquisitely detailed rules of ritual purity: contact with, in some instances even sight of, lower castes is viewed as polluting; intimate contact, especially in marriage or at meals, is especially defiling. "Scruples concerning purity are the keysone, or better the foundation stone, or all Hindu construction, and/... the parts are only ordered and kept in place by sentiments of pious respect and sacred horror" the fear of pollution is so intense that it not merely separates, but actually repels, castes from one another.

None of this is intended to suggest that questions of power and class can be ignored, let alone that purity is causally prior. Traditionally, however, purity, wealth and power have largely coincided. Purity offers the clearest entry into the philosophical and cultural logic of the castes system and allows us to treat the practice of castes according to its own terms of self justification. Furthermore, whether we adopt the Weberian notion of legitimacy or the Gramscian idea of hegemony, the ideological structure of instification must be a central part of the analysis of such a long lived and deeply ingrained social structure. Nevertheless, I do try to link ideas of purity directly to issues of power by considering tradional values as they were embedded and embodied in the actual practice of Hindu-dominated were embedded and embodied in the actual practice of Hindu-dominated India.

3. The ontology of caste: In the traditional Hindu world, all reality is one: Brahma, the absolute. 'Hinduism is a monistic religion which.... Believes in one ultimate spiritual reality or existence which reveals itself as this and many other worlds and is present everywhere in the universe and beyond it, and which dwells in every living being" Physical existence however, clouds one's recognition of this reality. Hinduism is "a unique life style concerned primarily with developing... the paradigmatic self aware man" and having achieved such awareness attaining ultimate and complete reunion with divine reality.

Everything is made of three basic gunas, three radical "substance" sattva, rajas, and tamas. Very roughly, sattva, the substance of purity resides in the mind, provides true knowledge of all reality as simply manifestations of Brahma, and is symbolized by the colour white; rajas, the substance of virility, resides in life itself, is associated with egoism, selfishness, and virulence, and is symbolized by the colour red; and tamas, the substance of dullness, resides in the body, gives rise to ignorance, and is symbolized by the colour black. Everything–deities, human beings, demons, animals, plants objects – is composed of these three substances but in different proportions: sattva predominates. In deities, rajas predominate in demons and animals, and tamas predominates in plants and objects. the cosmic hierarchy is replicated at the level of human society. Creating a fundamental "paralleism" between cosmic and social orders.

Hindu regards the nature and the cultural as non-dualistic features. Each is imminent in the other; each is inseparable from the other: each is a reflection of and realization of the other...

The entire.... Cosmos is ordered by a premise of ranked inequalities; all life forms within the cosmos are defined by the same radical material substances (gun) and the behavioural code dharma appropriate to those gun. The same is also, true, significantly .... Of human society of ordered ranks. And these birth-groups are destined according to the internal physical nature and the behavioural code held appropriate to that nature, which are viewed as a dupolex criterion of rank.

Placement in this social hierarchy, or caste system is by birth. Which according to the Hindu theory of reincarnation is not an accident or an arbitrary fact of nature, but a reflection of moral justice and order? "One is born where one belongs by reason of his actions over many incarnations" (Organ 1974:194). "The body or family in which a person is born, the society in which he lives, and the position or station in life which he occupies, are all determined by his past conduct and behaviour" (Chatter-Rebirht is an essential mechanism in the law of karma or punishment and reward for one's deeds.

Caste hierarchy thus "is the expression of a secret justice" "In a just and stable society a correspondence was presumed between a person's qualities and his social position" caste division and hierarchy are seen not as a matter of social convention but as part of the fabric of the universe. Caste reset on natural distinctions, not on social action; its justification is ontological and metaphysical, not functional. Both the hierarchical structure itself and the placement of each person within that structure rest on a divinely oriented natural order.

Thus, the very ideas of human nature is radically different in traditional Indian and in modern western though. In traditional India, human nature is not viewed as a common possession of all people. Rather, "Human nature." If we can even use that term without gross anachronism, differs from person to person – or rather, from group to group. "In Indian Thought, the caste is a species of making"

Birth and blood set only the upper limits of purity, however. Even for those born (relatively) Pure, pollution can easily come from one's own acts, even the most pure remain subject to the temptation of selfishness and physical desire, and even the most scrupulous remain vulnerable to violation by the others. Even mere contact with those less pure is polluting impurity is, as it were, contagious.

Caste and purity also serve as the basis of a functionally specialized division of labour, as seen in the frequent correspondence of caste and profession names. Anything connected with the body, especially with its wastes, is polluting; thus the low ranking of washers, sweepers, and scavengers. In fact, manual labour in any form is considered an inferior form of activity, and thus artisans and agricultural laboures are ranked below those, such as Brahman, who do not depends on labour. Occupation, life style and birth are therefore mutually reinforcing parts of a hierarchic social order of purity.

With a passion for the most subtle distinctions, traditina; India elaborated an incredibly varied and complex structure of castes and subcastes for example, we find intricate graduations among crafts; some artisans have relatively high status, while others lie at or near the bottom of the social hierarchy (particularly leather workers, who are untouchables because of the special religious significance of cattle). In agricultural as well tasks have differential ritual status or purity; plowing is especially degrading, in part because it is likely to involve killing insects and other lower life-forms, which have religion—moral value as bodily forms into which souls are born.

The "Secret justice" of caste, the intimate link between and mutual reinforcement of the type of life one leads and one's natural worth, gives social inequality a special moral significance. One's station has its duties(dharma) which are held to be perfectly suited to one's nature and the discharge of those duties, whatever they may be gives one a place in society and a certain personal dignity. Both the Bhagavad-Gita (3.35) and the laws of Manu (10.97) emphasize that it is better to perform one's own duties poorly. Even to die doing so , than to perform another's well and the proper discharge of the duties of one's station will be rewarded in the next life.

In practice, "inherited defilement" of membership in the lower castes has been the central social fact, but caste theoretically assures that each person is treated according to his or her desert and therefore can achieved a sort of contextual dignity. Therefore, the inequality and group repulsion of the social and ritual hierarchy maybe partially mitigated by the fact that all are bound together into an intricately articulated social and natural order. Each group is in part defined in part relation to the others and requires them Brahmans, for example, could not even survive without the services of other castes. The caste system in India represents an extreme form of Dukheiman organic solidarity, a social solidarity based on bringing together qualitatively different social groups, Brahma, the divine unity of all existence, provides an ontological and metaphysical point of reference toward which all reality aspires (to take extend that it is self aware). Likewise, the Brahman caste provides not merely a social point of reference purity in its broad outlines in perhaps most easily measured by the nature and extend of a caste's permissible contact with Brahmans—but the point towards which all social structures are directed and ultimately converge.

4. Flexibility, mobility and equality: The caste system of traditional India was an extraordinarily rigid social structure, but it was by means static. The proliferation of castes, which occurred principally through the fission of existing castes, involved considerable change. Reginald variations, not only in particular details but even if fairly substantial ways, such as the paucity of intermediate castes between Brahman and Sherri in southern India also suggest openness to evolutionary change.

Because purity rests on a combination of birth and act, downward mobility is a very real possibility; there are even jatis of "degraded Brahmans" who are shunned by the most other castes upward mobility is more problematic, however, special individual merit, though particularly dedicated performance of the duties of one's station or by becoming a religious ascetic, would be rewarded by a higher rebirth, but there was almost no way an individual could move to a higher caste in a single lifetime "Individual upward mobility, with the partial exception of hypergamous marriages, was virtually impossible.

Upward group mobility was also theoretically impossible, but in practice upward caste mobility, especially the local rise of a wealthy or powerful jati, has been a rare but real phenomenon throughout Indian history. "The reigning, ideal principle is that of social competition among those close to each other in rank," David mandelbaum presents a particularly though analytical account of the process of upward Jati mobility. The jati originmyuth is typically revised, usually to claim membership in achier Varna. This also provides a new behavioural model for the group. Srinivas refers to this process of lifestyle change as "Sankritization" In addition; social contacts are revised to reflect the new, aspired-to status. On its own, a jati can try to cut its contacts with groups that it now considers beneath itself. Much more important, thought, is acceptance into the new reference group: ultimately, one's children will have to acceptable as marriage partners or the "mobility drive" will fail.

Building alliances and patron client linkages—for example, by lending money or purchasing services over an extended period–can also be important. Securing the services and thus tacit recognition, of Brahmans or even lower superior castes is often a crucial step. For the mobility drive to success, wealth is necessary but "wealth alone...is no guarantee of higher rank. Jati members must use it property so that the jati's rank may be elevated for their children". In effect a materially successful jati can attempt to achieve "closer parity between a jati's secular powers and material resources". With some luck and considerable political skill, the jati can raise its status over the course of a few generations.

Such change, however, involve only relatively minor and local rearrangements of the parts; they leave the caste system untouched. The rising caste typically couches its claims almost entirely in reference to the traditional ideology, and once it has successfully raised it adopt the way of life of its new station and defends the immutability of caste divisions. This is a classic example of system maintenance by selective co-operation. Traditional India society could be remarkably flexible about particulars, but it was exceedingly unyielding about basis structures.

Even religious movement that began as hostile of Hinduism, either in general or in its "standard" Brahmanism version typically has fallen. Victim to reabsorption.

Mandelbaum discusses one common pattern; a charismatic leader teaching ideas of personal purity largely distinct from notions of caste and ritual becomes the leader of a social movement, which then is reabsorbed into dominant society as a new caste. This pattern is so common that standard complaint about such bhakti (devotinal) movements is that "in historical retrospect, their function appears to have been to reinforce the existing social order by channeling discontent into a negative form rather than bring about structural change" because no matter how spiritually egalitarian they are "theory tend to get organized and function within the existing socio - cultural order" and accept the existing hierarchy in secular contexts.

The absorptive power of Hinduaste society can also be seen in the penetration of caste ideas and practices into introduced religions, such as Islam and Christianity. Even more striking is the fact that Buddhism, a radically egalitarian religion that began in India, largely died out there and never seriously challenged the caste system. In fact, in some areas of southern Nepal there is even a Buddhist caste system.

Nonetheless, religious opposition to caste inequality, and the underlying social discount on which it must have flourished, should not be denigrated. "The burden on which its oppressive gradations, generated its own antithesis on the ideological plane, and the question of equability was insistently raised in a succession of religious movements that go back to the beginnings of recorded history". There would even seem to be at least some religious resources for reform within traditional Indian Hinduism for example, the doctrine of reincarnation impels a divine essence in each person doctrine that might be transformed in ways that are compatible with the idea of human right. Organ suggests that the notion of varnas should be read simply as an appropriate recognition of moral differences and those efforts at reform should focus on making it possible to move through the entire circuit and become a Brahman in a single life many reformers, including

Gandhi, have seen the fourfold varnascheme as remedy for the jati based caste system. Swami Nikhilanandra among many others has presented Hindu spiritualism as a remedy for many of the ills of modernity. And more examples could be added. In order words, in the contemporary struggle for human rights there may be important traditional cultural resources on which India can draw, but these resources lie at the fringes of a tradition dominated by the remarkably resilient caste system. If the practice of Human rights is to be realized in India, a radical break with tradition is required.

The radical incompatibility between caste and human rights is obvious, we, have already noted the social primary of duties over right in Indian, India also shares with other traditional societies a group orientation that is in contrast to the inherent individualism of viewing each person as possessing natural and inalienable right that ordinarily trace precedence even over the claims of society and the state, "Hindu society is organized around the concept of dharma (the duties of one's station) in a way roughly similar to modern society around that of the individual".

Perhaps even more important is the difference between the egalitarianism of human rights and the status orientation of the caste system that reflects a fundamentally different understanding of the moral significance of being human. Human rights "derive from the inherent dignity and worth that arise simply from being human, and thus each person has the same basic dignity; human rights are held equally by all. No less important, human worth and dignity is radically distinguished form the worth and dignity of the rest of creation human rights are radically different from the worth and dignity of the rights of all other beings.

The caste system, by contrast, denies the equal worth of all human beings. It draws sharp, qualitative moral distinctions between human beings other parts of creation. The human soul is not qualitatively different from that of beasts and even plants; it is only a somewhat more evolved (self-aware) incarnation. In fact, in many ways the distance between high castes and low castes is greater than that between lower castes and animals for example, the law of Manu prescribes the same penance whether a Brahman kills a cat, a mongoose, a blue jay, a frog, dog, iguana, owl crow, and considerably more attention is devoted to the crime of killed a cow, and considerably more attention is devoted to the crime of killing a cow than to killing a Shudra. "Dying without the expectation of a reward, for the sake of Brahmans and cows" will secure beatitude for Chandalas. In a following life, "the slay of a Brahman enters the womb of a dog, a pad, an ass, a camel, a cow, a goat, a sheep, a deer, a bird, a chandala..."

Given the traditional Hindu understanding of what it means to be a human being, the idea of human rights is a moral outrage, an affront to and attack on natural order and justice. Caste, the principal social expression of this understanding of human nature, must be forever antithetical to human rights.

A defender of caste point out that I have yet to shoe why we should not resolve the conflict by dismissing human as an alien incursion. Although human rights purport to be universal, the simple claim of universality provides no reason for those in another cultural to accept it. Therefore, we must pause to consider the counterclaims of cultural relativism, applying the general argument of Chapter 6 to the case of caste.

All Indian governments wince independence has rejected the caste system. Untouchability—which presents the most serious human rights problems that arise from the caste system. Those involving the grossest exploitation of roughly the bottom fifth of Indian society, the poorest of the poor in a very poor country—is central government and the separate states have long pursued a variety of relatively aggressive remedial legal, social, and economic programmes. Such official government policies, however, might be held to represent only the efforts of largely Westernized elite. In fact, the persistence of caste endogamy and caste-based patterns of social deference—especially in the country side, where most Indian live–might suggest that the rational caste system better reflect popular "human rights" value. But even if we were to grant that this is true, there are good reasons for pressing universal human rights arguments against caste.

We have already seen that the external human rights judgement of caste is in all respects negative. Should we abandon this eternal judgment just because caste has a long history and is deeply ingrained in Indian society? if the right violations inherent in the practice are of great external importance, it may be appropriate to press a negative external evaluation of even a very important an long–established culture practice. We should of cores, be wary of external moral judgemtns that contradict very important internal moral precepts, but when a large group of people are classified and traded as less than fully human, as they are in the caste system, we have crossed the boundaries of appropriate respect for eristic and self-determination.

In the case of India, the dangers of moral imperialism that may seem to lurk beneath pressing such as external evaluation are greatly reduced by the strong cross-cultural international consensus on the indefensibility of the caste system, the external judgment is not simply a 'western judgment', but one widely shared throughout the Third World as well. Furthermore, caste stands externally condemned not on the basis of a controversial interpretation of human rights or even the violation of just a few right, the Indian caste system violates virtually the full range of internationally recognized human rights, under all plausible interpretations of those rights. and this international consensus has considerable internal support, not only in the policies of Indian governments but also in the political activity of the victims of caste.

Caste is no longer "hegemonic," no longer accepted as legitimate especially but those at the bottom of the system, who increasingly see themselves as victims of oppression and exploitation. In such circumstances, cultural relativist arguments against international human rights standards must be decisively rejected as misguided at best and as little more than upper caste/class ideological subterfuge at worst. It may be necessary and even desirable to take persisting caste attitudes and practices into account when implementing internationally recognized human rights in India, but we must insist that the caste system and caste based domination give way to the demands of human rights, as the victims of caste are themselves increasingly demining in contemporary India.

Caste and the Contemporary Struggle for Human Rights

The preceding account of traditional Indian values is not merely of historical interest; attitudes and practices rotted in the ideas and institutions of the caste system remain of central importance in the struggle of human rights in contemporary India, especially in the countryside. But the caste system, the harmonic complex of caste ideas and practices, has eroded significantly.

Although caste still has great social, economic, and political relevance especially for rural untouchables the traditional coincidence of caste, class, and power is increasingly under attack, both indirect through the processes of economic modernization and political democracy, and directly through political action by and on behalf of untouchables and other "backward" or "depressed" communities. In fact, the struggle for the human rights of lower caste Indians can in many ways be seen as a struggle against the increasingly violent efforts of dominant castes, classes, and political elites to maintain the traditional correlation of caste, class, and power.

The principle challenge to the caste system has been and will continue tube economic change. In the countryside, the development of a money economy—and with it, increased opportunities for upward mobility by delinking wealth and traditional status—has weakened the relative power of

Brahman castes and radically altered traditional patron-client relations. In the cities, new jobs (filled in significant measure on the basis of merit, or at least of qualifications), new residential patterns, greater educational opportunities, and the missing of largely anonymous people on the streets, in buses, and in government offices have created important opportunities for at least some individuals to escape many of the burdens of caste.

Such tendencies have often been supported and strengthened by direct intervention by central and state governments. Untouchables is outlawed by Article 17 of the constitution, and the protection of Civil Rights Act (the 1976 successor to the unsociability gives special legal backing and enforcement to this prohibition. Bonded labour is similarly prohibited both by the constitution and by subsequent laws. Further-more, there are relatively aggressive programmes of what in the United States would be called "affirmative action," reserving places in educational institutions, jobs in the public sector, and even legislative seats for Untouchables, others Scheduled Castes, Scheduled Tribes, and other Backward classes. Special measures intended to benefit these depressed groups are also a regular feature of economic development and social service programmes. Land reform and minimum-wage measures as well have often been intended to benefit the lower castes. The efficacy of such political interventions and the vigor of state functionaries in applying the law are frequently open to questions, but the general tendency has been to hasten the erosion of the caste system.

The institutions and practices of political democracy which probably are as deeply rooted in India as in any other country in Asia, Africa, Latin, in the gram panchayats (village councils) and other local political bodies.

Non-Barman caste-Hindus usually have predominant power because of their economic, numerical, and political power. Representatives of the untouchables usually do not exercise substantial power, but simply their presences is often of social and psychological significance. The electoral power of non-bran groups at both the state level and the federal level has also been an important source of power and social change, especially as government grants and services play an ever-larger role in the economic and social life of both rural and urban communities. And electoral and local political activity has provided political skills, knowledge, and models for organizing and strengthening caste associations and grassroots political pressure groups.

It might be argued that in rural areas untouchables and other lower castes have to date been harmed at least as much as they have benefited from changes in both rural relations of production and the forms of elite political domination. national patron-client relations in India has been associated with an increasing concentration of resources and the denial of the benefits of traditional clientage, without the slack having been taken up by either the state or the market. As result, the landless in particular tend to end up even more excluded and more oppressed.

This particulary true given the widespread and flagrant disregard for such protective programmes as rural minimum wages. In travelling with a government labour officer in South Gujarat, Barman was not able to find a single work earning the statutory minimum wage; he computers the typical underpayment as equivalent to between one-forth and one-there of the labourer's annual income. But in 1983 and 1984, out of more than 27,000 inspections (virtually all of which must have tuned up violates of the law) only 82 cases (0.003%) were investigated and prosecuted to a conclusion. When Bremen questioned the responsible officials, it became clear that they and little interest in acting against offending employers. In fact, the chief of the load office plausibly claimed in his own defense that he was powerless to act because tough enforcement would be met by landlord violence against his officers.

The rise of private rural violence often with the acquiescence, collusion, or active support of the police, if a chilling and reality recent development. Traditional forms of rural social control, especially the caste-system, are losing their efficacy. Feeling challenged and threatened by economic change, government policies, a nod the growing assertiveness of depressed groups, rural elites have increasingly tended to work to overcome traditional (caste) divisions among themselves in the interest of maintaining a united front against the lower castes and classes, especially the landless (among whom untouchables are disproportionately represented) and super ordinate groups have increasingly turned to direct violence against per ordinate groups have increasingly turned to direct overt violence against depressed groups in order to maintain their control; "the landowners control the landless with intimidation and, when this fails, with outright terrorization".

In Bihar, terror campaigns have been carries out against peasants who have attempted to organize to protect their rights and interests. Three major caste-based "seas" (private armies)- Bhumi sea (used by kurmi landlords), Bramharsi Sena (Bhaumihars), and Larik Sena (Jadavs)- in collaboration with local dots (bandit gangs), have been used by landlords, often with the collusion of local authorities. Gujarat has as analogous problem with zim rakhas, "field guards, "usually hired by local landowners from urban gangs to keep the lower castes/ classes in line. Other areas have similar organization and even where the violence is less. Organized, it is a regular feature of rural economic and political relations and of course, such caste/class violence is only the most visible and dramatic evidence of an intense and multifaceted human rights struggle.

In the short run medium run, this new combination of more class like economic and political oppression probably leaves most of the traditional victims of the caste system little or no better off. Economic demographic, legal, and political changes have dramatically increased the social and economic opportunities available to some individual members of traditionally low status groups. These changes have also opened new opportunities for them to act politically to better their condition. But caste identification remains a central social reality; the struggle of traditionally oppressed groups for equality is being met by strong opposition from both old and new elites, and the groups traditionally at the bottom of the social hierarchy still remain, for the most part, at the bottom.

The struggle against caste and its legacies remains at the center of the struggle for human rights in India, but we must be careful not to equate the two, particularly to the extent that caste, class, and political power have become separate based of domination. Difficult and momentous as it is, the struggle against caste will not be the end of the struggle for human rights in India. It may not even be the decisive phase. To free landless untouchable India. It may not even be the decisive phase. To free landless untouchable agricultural laborers, for example, from the stigma of untouchability—to truly, not just legally, free them, so that they not others would identify them as untouchables—would be a major victory, a decisive break with a grossly oppressive traditional practice. But unless these labourers are able to obtain ownership of land, a fair wage and good working conditions, or access to a decent urban or industrial job, unless they are able to organize, economically and politically without fear of official and unofficial violence and harassment; and unless their human rights will continue to be violated—in a new form, but no less surely. Class oppression is different from caste oppression but it is no less oppression.

The real human rights question in is not whether caste dominantation is to be replaced, but what is to replace it. Although still powerful, the caste system, in its traditional form, is on the decline. This significant advance must be purchased further with all possible speed and energy, but overthrowing the caste system is not enough, nay more than overthrowing imperialism sufficed. The struggle against caste in India must be evaluated both by how far India has moved away from the caste system and by how close it has moved toward implementing human rights–two important and perhaps even related, but distinct, directions of social change.

Human Rights as Education for Peace

Peace education, a worldwide movement, is a diverse and continually changing field, responding to developments in world society extent, to the advancing knowledge and insights of peace research. As practiced in elementary and secondary schools and presented in the university programmes that prepare classroom teachers, peace education goes by various names: conflict resolution, multicultural education, development education, world order studies, and more recently, environmental education. Each of these approaches responds to a particular set of problem that has been perceived as the causes of social injustice, conflict, and war. Each could also be classified as "preventive education" as it seeks to prevent the occurrences of the problems that inspire it more important; each is conceived as education of a set of social values. Although each relates to peace in the sense of social cohesion and the avoidance of the form of violence to which it responds, none of them displays the elements of prescription and holism so essential to understanding the increasingly nonfactual interdependent, planetary social system from which peace is to be wrought. Each is primarily responsive, particularistic and problem focused.

Peace Education Needs Human Rights Education

Even that strand peace education that sees itself devoted specifically to learning's about "peacemaking" has been primarily problem-centered, focusing of "negative peace." The reduction, avoidance, and elimination of warfare. As such, it has been devoted more to a study directed toward eliminating the causes of war than to creating the conditions of peace, more too negative circumstances of what should not be than to the possibilities of what could be. So it is that peace education and peace studies (as the fields is known in universities) have been a bit of a "downer" for all but those students who are either "positive thinkers" by nature, drawn to social action fields, or simply curious about the study of the "impossible". Thus peace education as such is less viable in/ American secondary and elementary schools than the other approaches enumerated here, which have immediate relevance to community concerns. And only a small fraction of university students ever pursue courses in peace studies, even though they are now offered in several hundred institutions of higher education. While not entirely attributable to its responsive, particularistic, and problematic nature, the fact that it is a minority, not a majority, of students who receive peace education may well be a serious a obstacle to the peace-making capacities of this country that does not actively educate its citizens for peace. This assumption underlies the central argument put forth here that human rights educations is not only corrective complement to education for peace but that is essential to the development of peace-making capacities and should be integrated into all forms of peace education. It is through human rights education that learners are provided with the knowledge and opportunities for specific corrective action that can fulfil the prescriptive requirements of education for space.

Human rights education, fast becoming another global educational phenomenon, appears to be developing along equally varied, but more substantively focused and prescriptive lines. It comprehends some of the same normative goals espoused by peace education, provides a dimension of concrete possibilities for alternatives to current world conditions and offers a constructive action dimension to complement and apply to all the diverse forms of peace education. Many recent world developments similar to those that have produced the existing approaches to peace education have been articulated as human rights issues and problems, so that some peace educators are adding human rights to the list of approaches. While the addition is certainly necessary, it is far from deficient and fails to exploit the essential contribution that human rights can make to peace education, namely providing the basis for a prescriptive, holistic yet particularized approach that would make peace education not only more comprehensive but also far more comprehensible. The actual human experiences that comprise much of human rights education are more readily understood than the theoretical and analytical concept of peace education.

The conceptual core peace education is violence, its control, reduction, and elimination. The conceptual core of human rights education is human rights origination, fulfilment, and universalization. As I have raged elsewhere, human rights are most readily adaptable to the study of positive peace, the social political and economic conditions most likely to provide the environment and process for social cohesion and nonviolent conflict resolution. This essay contends that education for peace should route through which to move problem to prescription in all the various approaches to peace education. Positive peace, conceptualized by the peace research community to extend the definition of peace beyond the limitation, avoidance, or absence of war to include issues of justice, poverty, and freedom is the concept of peace that is the foundational principle of the Universal Declaration of Human Rights. The inextricable relationship between human rights and peace is articulated in the very first sentence of the preamble to the Declaration, "recognition of the inherent dignity and of the equal and inalienable rights of all members of the human family is the foundation of freedom, justice, and peace in the world." Since the core and seminal document for all current standards of human rights, to which all members of the Unites nations are assumed to assent, acknowledges this principle, surely education for peace should also do so. Certainly, both peace researchers and activists and human rights scholars and advocates can agree that violence in all its forms is an assault on human dignity.

Peace research now recognizes several particular forms of violence as the conceptual rubrics under which data are gathered and knowledge derived: physical or behavioural violence including war and other uses of direct force to destroy or weaken or otherwise harm another nation, group, or individual; structural violence, which refers to the poverty and deprivation that results from in just and inequitable social and economic structures; the political violence of oppressive systems that enslave, intimidate, and abuse dissenters as well as the poor, powerless, and marginalized; and cultural violence the devaluing and destruction of particular human identities and ways of life, the violence of racism, sexism, ethnocentrism, colonial ideology, and other forms of moral exclusion that rationalize aggression, domination, inequity and oppression. All these forms of violence can be made most apparent and comprehensible within a human rights framework. Analyzing these forms of violence as violations of particular human rights frame work. Analyzing these forms of violence as violations of particular human rights standards provides a constructive alternative to presenting them as abstract concept, as is often the case in peace education. It is for just such reasons that some educators teaching in the fields for conflict resolution, multiculturalism, development education, and world order studies and a limited number of environmental educators are now integrating human rights issues and standards into their curricula as subject matter content, as perspectives for the development of critical capacities, and as areas for experiential learning. To each of these forms of peace education, human rights bring not only the element of concrete experience and observable social conditions but also a much needed normative and prescriptive dimension.

Each has acknowledged a concern with values formation and ethical decision-making process that have been problematic in a educational system, somewhat ambivalent on the subject of values and ethics, alternately purporting to be value free and/or to encourage consideration of contending values and value system, while in actuality conveying the unarticulated and unexamined prevailing values of the society, mainly ignoring the ethical questions imbedded in social issues. This confusion in education is readily the ethical questions imbedded in social issues. This confusion in education is readily reflected in the contradictions in public policy and in the limited capacities of citizens to make policy judgments. Conflict resolution is probably the most widely practiced approached to peace education in American elementary and secondary school. The approach is mainly one that emphasizes processes and techniques for dealing with small group and interpersonal conflict. Teachers of these techniques often introduced to overcome problems of classroom discipline, playground fights, and some of the more serious forms of violence that now plague our public education system, try to communicate the values of fairness and demonstrate the efficacy of nonviolence. However, like the wider field of dispute resolution, the orientation of the instruction tends to be pragmatic rather than explicitly normative or ethical.

Specific and often very effective skills are taught which enable a third party of the disputants themselves to reach a resolution acceptable to both or all parties to the dispute. The emphasis is on the achievement of an acceptable resolution in terms of the particular elements of the immediate dispute. It is rare, at least, in elementary and secondary education that consideration of the roots or the long-range consequences of the conflict are brought into process. Most conflict resolution education, as generally practiced, does not teach students to understand structural and systemic aspects of conflict, and only in a few cases comprehends the cultural elements of conflict, thus overlooking value issues.

Yet this lack in no way devalues the skills that are taught, they are of lifelong relevance to all forms of experience, interpersonal as well as social and political. Conflict resolution training certainly has had dramatically positive results in the schools where it is offered. And these results argue well for such skill development to be a required instructional goal of all our schools if we truly desire them to be peaceful and democratic learning environments. It does, however, indicate that while necessary to peace education, the study of conflict resolution is not sufficient to its purpose of providing learning's that will contribute to fundamental and long-range change to reduce violence substantially by increasing social justice and respect for human dignity.

Were this skills training and its attitudinal bases, which incorporate the values of reason, open communication, and fundamental fairness to use principles of human rights as the criteria of fairness, conflict resolution could offer a more integrated and comprehensive approach to peace education. For example, examining causes and long-range effects of conflicts interims of violations and fulfilment of human rights would provide an excellent basis for the clarification of the values of equity and fairness and the application of principles of justice. Some of the most sever and violent conflicts are caused by actual or perceived violations of human rights. In looking at whatever conflict of process that is being studies in the framework of the recognition, fulfilment, and universalization for human dignity, students can come to understand the differences between constructive conflicts; to appreciate how nonviolently conducted conflict has often been the means to overcome injustice and achieve more truly peaceful social orders; and to understand that conflict is a significant process in all social change. For peace education, the purpose of teaching the skills of conflict resolution is to widen the possibilities for preventing conflicts from honour human dignity.

In this regard, the theme and principles of non-violence, the focus of some peace education, could be used as a conceptual framework for conflict resolution and as a normative approach to teaching about social change, political strategy, and modern history. It could also illuminate how the commitment to human dignity that is the essence of nonviolence inspires the struggle for human rights as the basis for overcoming the many forms of violence that impede a viable, just peace. This commitment requires consistence between means and ends. Violence, the ultimate insult human dignity, is not a suitable means through which to struggle for its realization. Human rights, "the how and the who" of potential violations that could result from a given means, are an excellent tool for determining whether those means are truly nonviolent.

The study of various ethnic groups and cultural has become a major focus in education at all levels, producing certain controversies as it seeks to respond to others. There are two major wellsprings of this stream of peace education. The first was in the recognition of the need for understanding other cultures resulting from the realities of international inter depends and the necessity of international cooperation to address global problems. This source emphasized the study of the cultures of other parts of the world, giving little attention to the variety of cultures within nations. This omission, particularly as it did little to challenge the Eurocentime of most American curricula, was one impetus for the second wellspring, the ethnic consciousness movements of the 1970s and 1980s, which became the social equivalents of the civil rights movements of the 1950s and 1960s. As conflict resolution was a response to communal and school disturbance (often caused by ethnic tension and conflicts) multicultural studies was a response to change in immigration patterns and the reawakening of cultural identities long presumed to have been subordinated to one common national identity. The "hyphenated Americans" included the recently arrived from Asia, Latin America, and Eastern Europe and the descendants of European and African peoples many generations in the United States. In an essentially racist society, few of these groups were fully at peace with or adequately acquainted with the values and traditions of others. As the interests of group came more openly into conflict, the necessity of such understanding proved to be as essential to domestic tranquility as international understanding was deemed to be to world peace. Experiences similar to this were evident, as well, in the former socialist countries where ethnic conflicts produced armed conflicts (*e.g.*, Yugoslavia and Amenia), some of them, like those in Africa and Asia, genocidal proportions.

Cross-cultural ignorance and the hostilities it helps to maintain and exacerbate argue strongly for multicultural education as an essential elements of education for peace. The atrocities that characterize the conflict fed by the ethnic hostilities demand that human rights be central to any education directed towards intercultural understanding. Indeed, some educators would argue that respect for and knowledge of cultures are essential to the realization of human rights should be the essential ethical core of such understanding not only to prevent violence but to assure an adequate and effective process of peace-making not only to prevent violence but to assure an adequate and effective process of peace-making.

Indeed, ethnic conflict demonstrate perhaps more clearly than any other conflicts that human rights should be guiding criteria not only for conflict resolution but for all aspects and phases of a peace-making process. Particularly in the negotiations of settlement and the establishment of the terms of peace among conflicting ethnic groups, human rights principles should be used to assure the parties of the fairness of the agreements. Within the peace processes of peace-keeping, peace-making and peace-building outlined by the secretary general of the United Nations, human rights standards would be an invaluable tool in all phase. They could be used in decision-making about peace-keeping actions, and guide peace-making negotiations toward outcomes that would be inherently more just a thus most significantly viable. It is in the area of peace-building, creating the conditions for peaceful relationships, that preparation in multicultural understanding informed by human rights concepts could make a significant contribution to the formation of the peace-makers and the public's that must support their efforts. These specific aspects of the most significant recent proposals for a peace-making process demonstrate that multicultural education fused with human rights education is essential not only to those charged with carrying out the process, but to the citizens of all nations need such education in these years when the United States is the major "player" in peace-keeping, it is an urgent necessity.

Human rights concepts and principles can also be used to achieve what has been the major instructional goal of multicultural education: developing the capacity to understand, clarify, and appreciate similarities and differences among cultures. Such comparisons are not intended to judge one culture as ethically superior to any other or others. Aversion to the notions of cultural superiority and cultural relativism, combined with an acknowledged commitment to equity among peoples, makes peace educators sensitive to such judgment. Yet the field is a value centered one and has been much in need of a value system that does not do disservice to the value of pluralism fundamental to cultural equity and diversity. Human rights, as enumerated in the Universal Declaration and the international standards, provide the framework for comparisons and assessment of the human condition on the basis of the most global criteria available. Although primarily western in origin, these standards have a sufficient degree of authentic universality to have been generally accepted as human values, the core principles of which are adaptable to most cultures. Indeed, such was a major conclusion of the 1993 Vienna world conference of Human Rights. Although disputed by authoritarian government, the principle of universality is globally recognized by Human Rights movements and, more significantly, by most UN member states, even some of those in contention with the movements.

Study of the myriad modes cultures use to implement rights could provide concrete instruction about the variety of possibilities a culturally diverse world has for honouring human dignity, pursuing human values, and fulfilling human needs. This in itself is an essential lesson in peace education, which seeks to develop the consideration of multiple alternatives in an effort to determine which among various policies, proposals; and behaviours are most conducive to the achieve-ments of peace and justice. Cross-cultural study of human rights concepts could be the vehicle for learning about how cultures vary in the structures of human and social relationship and ways of according respect to the human person; how human identity and dignity is experienced in different contests, both individual and communal. A major purpose of such inquiry is to demonstrate not only variety and differences, but the possibilities of what cultures can learn from each other about what it is to be human.

Using human rights concepts and standards in multi-cultural education can provide the essential basis for teaching reasons valuing and judgment making. The standards in their derivation and application involve both principles that are universal and practices that are culturally and contextually particular. Learning to recognize and differentiate between principle and practice involve skills as important to peace-making capacities as are the skills of conflict resolution. By observing how some principles can be practiced in a variety of ways, students can gain not only lessons about how cultural diversity could flourish within a system of common social ethics, but also within what contexts and circumstances value judgments regarding cultural practices are valid and defensible.

The use of the standards in such study is intended to provide reference points and general principles. Each of the general principles of the Universal Declaration of Human rights can provide a basis for searching out cultural norms and practices that implement or deny the principles. Distinctions could be made between the actual social institutions, practices, and conditions and the cultural beliefs and values in which they are embedded. Such learning includes, of course, tolerance of differences and cross cultural understanding, but also the limits of the acceptability or tolerability of social conditions that cause any human suffering that can be classified as violence. The legal standards of the covenants and conventions can be used to assess tolerability how the societies, particularly the political and economic systems in which the people of the various cultures live, measure up to the standards.

Here is another major point inseparability human right and the forms of peace education intended to contribute to their achievement. It is in the assessment of tolerability and acceptability that the notion of violence converges with that of human dignity. Violence, for the purpose of peace education, has been defined as unnecessary, avoidable, or international harm. When human dignity is assaulted in any way by social institutions, norms, or behaviours that are, or purport to be, sanctioned by the values and worldviews of the culture, the resulting harm is described as cultural violence.

It is readily evident from the limited study of this form of violence that peace research has thus for conducted that few cultures are free of it. While the degrees of severity may vary from one society to another, tests a global phenomenon. It is one factor that enables us to conceive of human rights as universal aspirations and common standards of achievement for all people and all nations.

The notion of a "common standards of achievement" provides avenues for the consideration of international cultural change as a long range, comprehensive strategy for the universal fulfilment human rights, the kind of strategy that has informed the women's and antiracist movements. Inquiry into such change and the requisite strategies has long been pursued in peace education. Although the areas for remedial action on behalf of human rights are primarily legal political, it is becoming evident that the most egregious violations are often the consequence of deep-rooted cultural beliefs and tardyons. The most vivid and, to many women, the most apparent of these are the beliefs and traditions of patriarchy. Clearly sexism, racism and cadaverous other forms of authoritarian oppression have been rationalized oven centuries by appeal to particularistic interpretations of the most revered authority sources of the cultures of the societies in which they have flourished. Yet both have been universally denounced as antithetical to human dignity in international instruments drafted by the United Nations and accepted by most world cultures. These denunciations, it needs to be emphasized, have been for the most part the consequences of social movements organized and carried out by victims of the indignities and their advocates not governments. Such movements are the consequences of social learning's we would now classify as human rights as education. Although some governments way come into power as a consequence of human rights initiatives and movements, they are not the initiators or the movers, they are the moved. States have crafted and agreed to human rights standards under the pressure and inspiration of other forces. For the most part, states are still major obstacles to the fulfilment of human rights, being primarily and sometimes exclusively motivated by their obsessions with their own perpetuation.

Thus human rights standards can be taught as the concepts of dignity and justify and acknowledge social wrong and cultural faults, as the guidelines through which societies can conceptualize and pursue cultural changes, and as the impetus to governmental action to defend of citizens, action that requires that governments, too receive human rights education.

It is especially important in the study in the cultures to provide and understanding that cultures, like all things human, evolve and change. They respond to their environments and adapt to survive. In the global age, in which the unity of humankind is as much a pragmatic necessity an ethical imperative, the universal standards of human rights provide the most obvious and effective guidelines for cultural changes. Here it is to underlined that such change, while it can be influenced, even inspired, by other cultures and international society, is only legitimate and actually effective when embraced and propelled by the peoples of the cultures concerned. It is necessary that those peoples intended to change their culture should be changed, and design the learning strategies to devise the changes deemed necessary.

Here, too, women's issues, especially such culturally sensitive questions as marriage and reproductive rights, are goods cases in point. Whereas specific global standards are both necessary and useful, the ways in which they are implemented need to be decided and applied by those directly concerned. Such issues offer excellent instructional opportunities for reflection on how principles that respect the unity of humankind, the integrity of the various and distinct human cultures, and the dignity of the human person could be formulated and applied in a global society. They also shoe how all those involved in the designated social wrong must be educated to change themselves and the situations that violate rights. For example, both women and men must be involved in such education relating to women's rights.

Development Education

Development education as an approach to education for peace has focused on the economic inequites between the rich nations and the poor. The systematic undermining of the well-being of the peoples of the poor nations imposed by the present global economy are classified as structural violence. The structures, institutions and policies of the present economic system limit the length and debase the quality of life of the majority of the human family that inhabits the poor countries of "the South".

Peace-oriented development education inquires into the consequences of these structures and potential alternatives to them, placing special emphasis on the responsibilities of the nation of "the North," whose wealth and power enable them to virtually control the system. In that these states are "representative democracies," their citizens also bear responsibility. Social and personal responsibility is key notions of human rights education. As peace education has addressed this issue with regard to war crime and crimes against humanity, so too, development education might address it in relation to the violation of economic and social rights that are life and death questions for millions.

All forms of development education could be enhanced by the incorporation of human rights as goals and standards. They can be used as the basis for reflection on the needs for and the efficacy and desirability of modes and purposes of economic and social development and the roles of the North and South in carrying them out. A Major drawback to development education has been what some educators have claimed is a stance of "noblesse Oblige" and therefore superior to the 'Less-developed" or "underdeveloped" nations. The core questions put to students are about how much and under what circumstances the "developed" nations should "contribute" to the "developing" nations. There are few or no questions as to the source and justice of the North's control over the resources from which they make their contributions to the south.

Even those curricula and programmes that are presented in terms of global social justice rather than charitable sharing of bounty tend towards motivating learners in the North to want to "help" and those in the south to want to "Progress" were development education to be presented primary in the context of issues related to facilitating the equitable fulfilment of social and economic rights, these attitudes of condescension and "boot strapping" might be avoided. The inquiry could look into the origins of economic and social rights in such a way as to demonstrate how the recognition to the rights of industrial workers was a contributing factor to the development of the industrial capacities that led to the North gaining control of the South. The future of these rights and changes in human rights concepts could also be explored. The concept of the "right to development" is an excellent introduction to the notion that communities of people as well as individuals are the subjects of rights. In that the evolution of these standards is current and highly political, the concept of group rights can also be used to teach the dynamics of the ongoing process of identifying and remediation obstacles and insults to human dignity that constitutes the global human rights movements.

Human rights can bring to development education the notion development as a process of the evolution of a society based upon normative principles that call for the fulfilment of economic, social, and cultural rights through the elimination of avoidable poverty and the equitable distribution of whatever benefits a society may possess. Some refer to this process as "social development," a process through which societies become more responsive to the needs and dignity of all their members. This is the concept of development most consistent with the principles of the universality and indivisibility of human rights, a concept best communicated by a holistic or comprehensive approach to education for peace.

World Order Studies

World order studies, developed from inquiries into war prevention and concern with physical, particularly armed, violence is the approach to education for peace that has included explicit study of human rights since its inception. Human rights has been one of the major substantive areas of world order studies which defines itself as an inquiry into the realization of a set of global values. It focuses on the possibilities for alternative security systems and international institutions more adequate to the realization of the values and the resolution of multiple global crises. It pays special attention to inter linkages among and between world problems and to the capacities of international law to resolve them. Thus it has considered the relationships between militarism and political repression, between arms expenditures and the deprivation of social and economic well-being, and more recently the coincidence of ecological destruction and the plight of indigenous people. The international law of human rights has relevance to this field because of the institutional problems it addresses and the normative nature of the approach. These are characteristics that confine it to the upper secondary and university levels of formal education.

World order studies pioneered the integration of the concepts of "alternative futures" and "relevant utopias" into peace curricula, and introduced a problem solving approach that emphasized the application of the "world order values" to the assessment of alternative institutional and policy proposals for the prevention of war and achievement of positive peace. Because of this value framework, the approach can be even further enriched by the development of human rights education, just as it has something of significance to offer to that development.

One of the barriers to the involvement of secondary and no specialist students in world order studies is the abstract and theoretical nature of most of the discourse, particularly as it pertains to actual and potential international institutions.

Human rights issues can bring an element of the lived human experience to the consideration of institutional issues. Case material on human rights abuses and specific struggles for justice presented as challenges to be met in the design and pursuit of institutional changes can enliven the study with factual knowledge of what needs to be changed, and with concrete examples of how present institutions actually affect people's lives.

Introducing the institutional issues is a contribution that world order studies can make to human rights education. Both the world order and human rights movements find national sovereignty to be a major impediment to the achievement of their espoused goals. Human rights education, however, has yet to exploit the pedagogical possibilities of "relevant utopias," proposal for institutional and systematic change that could alter the present system of sovereign nation-states so as to increase the possibilities for the fulfilment of human rights. And little attention is given to the institutions' processes for remediation of human rights abuses. For example, students might be called upon to consider how nation states or human rights organizations and might be called upon to consider how nation states or human rights organizations and activists should respond to human rights abuses, but now how international standards and legal remedy could be applied, or how to change to transform the international systemic which the abuses take place. Questions about how to assure an order that upholds human rights, an order called for by article 28 of the Universal Declaration of human Rights, still receive inadequate attention in human rights education. Human rights education could be made more adequate to the needs of educating to make judgments on international institution and policies by adapting this leaf from the world order studies book.

The inquiry that might be derived from bringing together the structural issues of world order and the ethical questions of human rights presents a core question from which a significant new dimension can be brought to each field. What are the possible structural and institutional changes that might effectively reduce violence and promote human dignity world social system? The questions that follow could serve to guide the development of curricula that could achieve the purposes of both fields of study. These questions would address indicators of violence and dignity, study of these indicators would, of course, involve the international human rights standards, further questions to explore the kinds of political process and citizen's movements that could promote institutional change would include study of human rights organizations and initiatives throughout the world. Thus the range of agents capable of acting for human rights and peace beyond nation-states and international organizations would be included, promoting a fuller and more accurate picture of the present system and the possibilities to change it. Such an inquiry would also open to secondary and university student's opportunities for action, specific ways in which they could exercise the responsibilities of global citizenship.

Environmental Education

Finally, a few comments on an approach only a few consider to be education for peace, yet one that may present the greatest opportunity of an integrated, comprehensive education for peace. Environmental education, developed by those who view the problem from planetary and ethical perspectives has much in common with comprehensive peace education in its systemic analysis and its value based inquiry. Perceived by many as "nonpolitical," it provided a convenient and fruitful basis for educational collaboration among educators who might otherwise have been deterred from direct cooperation on more apparently political topics. Such a collaboration between American and Soviet educators in the warning years of the cold war produced a new approach to comprehensive peace education, "ecological and cooperative education."

This is an approach that brings an ecological or living systems perspective to the study of global problems, and apples the pedagogy of cooperative learning to develop urgently needed capacities for social integration. It also brings up possibilities for the application of human rights principles to subjects even wider than social, ethnic, or national groups. It provides a way of considering the possibility that the human species as a unit has rights, a possibility implied in the designation of some human rights abuses as "crimes against humanity". The question of who may claim the right to a healthful environment has stymied those who would make such a claim for individuals or even for groups in the class actions. There are no way separate or draw borders between "sections" of the environment. It is an organic unity and can only be effectively addressed as such. A claim made to environmental rights would of necessity have to comfier the whole environmental system, the planet and the living system that comprise it. (The failure to recognize has been a factor that obstructs reason and clarity in environmental debates.)

The claim would also require consideration of responsibility that would, given out knowledge of how unregulated individual behaviours cumulatively affect the environment, need to be defined just as comprehensively. If humankind has rights, does it not also have responsibilities, and through what agents might that responsibility be exercised? Such is a question of populations, which can only be addressed by the planetary generation, those born to an Earth seen from space as a whole and living planet. It is a question that, more than any other, will determine their future. From teaching experience, I know that they recognize and respond that question.

Ecological and cooperative education points to the direction in which education for peace is now moving, and it can be argued, should move. If than directions is to lead to a humanly viable and ethically tolerable (even if temporary) destination, should know the movement be guided by the principles and standards of human rights? It each approach can be made more effective by the inclusion of human rights, then human right must be central to any comprehensive, integrated approach. Peace education and human rights education in their present forms are but different starting points to the same intended destination, a more just and peaceful world.

REFERENCES

1. "Preventive Education," Unesco Sources 57 (April 1994), monthly dossier, pp. 7-16.
2. Betty Reardon, *Education for Human Dignity; Learning About Rights and responsibilities:* A.K-12 Teaching Resource (Philadelphia: University of Pennsylvania Press, 1955).
3. Morton Deutech, *The Resolution of Conflict: Constructive and Destrucitive Process* (New Haven, Conn: Yale University Press, 1973).
4. James Banks, *Multiethnic Education: Theory and Practice* (Boston: Allyn and Bacon, (1988).
5. UN General Assembly, Report to the Secretary-General on the Work of the Organization, *An Agenda for Peace: Preventive Diplomacy, Peacemaking and Peace keeping,* UN Doc. A/47/277S/24111(June 17, 1992).
6. Universal Declaration of Human Rights, Para 1.
7. The materials and approaches to development education most appropriate to a human rights perspective have been and are being devised by the United Nations Children's Fund (UNICEF).
8. Betty Reardon, *Comprehensive Peace Education* (New York: Teachers College Press, 1987).
9. Richard Falk, Robert Johansen, and Samuel Kim, *The Constitutional Foundations of Work Peace* (Albany: State University of New York Press, 1993).
10. Betty Reardon, and Eva Nordland, *Learning Peace; The Promise of Ecological and Comparative Education* (Albany: State University of New York Press, 1994).

Human Rights, National Security and Terrorism

Who would have thought that India would need to tutor Australia on protecting individual human rights? Yet here we have the case of the Government of India summoning the Ambassador of Australia to remind his Government of the need for due process in the treatment of an Indian doctor detained in Brisbane.

The case highlights the importance of proper balance between civil liberties, individual human rights, and the responsibility of the state to protect inhabitants from terrorists. Before 9/11, western governments and human rights champions were prone to moral ambivalence between perpetrators of terrorism and efforts of legitimate governments to maintain national security and assure public safety. After 9/11 western governments began to view other countries parallel wars against terrorism through the prism of a fellow government facing agonizing policy choices in the real world, rather than single-issue groups whose vision is not anchored in any responsibility for policy decisions. Many governments used to be at the receiving end of moral and political judgment about robust responses to violent threats posed to their authority and order from armed dissidents. They now get a more sympathetic hearing and mature understanding forged in the crucible of shared suffering.

This does not give any government a license to trample rights won at great cost over many centuries: rights of people against government. A human right, owed to every person simply as a human being, is inherently universal. Held only by human beings, but equally by all, it does not flow from any office, rank or relationship. The language of human rights embodies the intuition that the human species is one and every individual is entitled to equal more consideration. It is vividly captured in the Second World War joke that they came after the workers; I was not a worker, so I did not object. They came after the homosexuals: I wasn't one, so I did not object, they came after the Jews; I wasn't one, so I did not object, then they came after me: There was no one left to object.

Success in defeating terrorism can come only if we remain true to values that terrorists reject. It is possible to resort to the lesser evil of curtailing liberties and using violence in order to defeat the grater evil of terrorism, but only if we do not succumb to the greater evil of destroying the very values for which democracies stand.

The way to this is to require of Governments that they justify all restrictive measures publicly, submit them to judicial review, and circumstances them with sunset clauses to guard against the temporary becoming permanent. The safeguards are especially important because the history of the great democracies themselves suggests that most people privilege the security of the majority over the harm done to minorities deprived of their rights in the name of national security.

After 9/11, some western democracies recalibrated the existing balance between national security and civil liberties in their laws and practices. American priorities shifted to subordinate human rights to victory in the 'war' against terrorism. A counter terrorism expert testified that "After 9/11 the gloves came off" while another official remarked that "if you don't violate someone's human rights, you aren't doing your job". There developed also the distasteful practiced of "rendition to torture". Sending prisoners to their home countries precisely because the alter were known to practice torture as a routine part of their interrogation.

Many other democracies jointed the United States in shifting the balance of laws and administrative practices towards state security. In Australia, the post 9/11 hysteria was harvested by the Government to introduce tough detention laws against illegal immigrants in defense of a policy of Fortress Australia that led to the detention of dozens of Australian citizens, one whom was deported to her country of birth and another, a mentally ill woman, spent ten months in detention.

Thus terrorism has an impact on human rights in three ways. First, it is itself an extreme denial of the most basic human right, namely to life, and it creates an environment in which people cannot live in freedom from fear and enjoy their other rights. Secondly, the threat of terrorism can be used by governments to enact laws that strip away many civil liberties and political freedoms. One simple yet popular technique is to reverse the burden of proof; those accused of terrorist activities sympathies or even guilt by association on the basis of accusations by anonymous people are to be presumed to be guilty until they can prove their innocence of unspecified charges. Thirdly, without necessarily amending laws or enacting new ones, governments, can use the need to fight terrorism as an alibi to stifle dissent and criticism and imprison or threaten domestic opponents.

This is where the case of Dr. Mohamed Haneef is so very disturbing. On the evidence presented to the Brisbane court, he made the mistake of giving his prepaid SIM card to a second cousin in the United Kingdom because the card would not be of any use to him in Australia for whose sunny shores he was departing. The card was found in a car used by a terrorist a year later.

Hardly surprising that the magistrate granted bail. This is where the case gets cruiser and curioser as Alice remarked in her wonderland. Having spent 12 days in custody before being questioned, then grated bail pending trail, Dr. Haneef had his multiyear work visa canceled on 'Character' grounds.

No country will strip its immigration Minister of the power to cancel a visitor's visa. But the purpose is to prevent someone from entering or, if he is already in the country, to terminate his presence and deport him. In Dr. Haneefs case the primary motivation would appear to be to keep him in Australia under detention-and require him to pay for the privilege at the end of it all, even if he should be acquired.

To top it all, the government has made it clear that Dr. Haneef will be deported even if he is ultimately found innocent. A case perhaps of guilty even if proven innocent?

It is hard not to infer that this is a case of serious misuses of power and political interference in the process of criminal justice.

The dream of a world ruled by law is a shared vision. We must not privilege security and order to such an extent as to destroy our most cherished values of liberty and justice in the search for an unattainable absolute security. As Benjamin Franklin, one of the fathers of American independence, said, those who would sacrifice essential liberty to temporary safety deserve neither liberty nor safety.

The robustness and resilience of the civilised world's commitment to human rights norms and values will be judged in the final analysis not be the breaches in the aftermath of 9/11, but by the reversal and attenuation of the breaches through judicial and political processes as well as the pressure of domestic and international civil society. This is where the response of the Australian community to the prima facie abuse of executive power of the Australian Government is so reassuring the legal fraternity, civil liberties groups, other sectors of society, an even the state premier have either roundly condemned the extra judicial detention of detention of Dr. Haneef or demanded a public explanation from the government. The one disappointment has been the federal opposition labour party, which frightened of being wedged on an issue of national security, has once again resorted to "metooism".

If and when Dr. Haneef is tried in a court of law, the trail will be about him : his beliefs, actions, and links to terrorism. The manner, forum, and rules of procedure of the trial are not about him, but about the quality and credibility of the Australian justice system, specifically, do the Australian Government belief in, respect and abide by the rule of law or disregard it as a mere inconvenience when judicially tested? The question of indifference or active concern about Dr. Haneef's fate in a foreign land is about Indian values and beliefs. A failure by the Government to demand justice for him would be an abdication of its responsibility to protect citizens.

Tough on terrorists, Tougher on the causes of terrorism. But toughest of all on safeguarding the virtues of tolerance, human rights, civil liberties, and due process.

(Ramesh Thakur, Distinguished Fellow at the centre for international Governance Innovation and Professor of Political Science at the University of Waterloo in Canada, is an Australian citizen).

Essentials of Negotiation

The Mind and the Heart

In 1998, the National Basketball Association (NBA) owners initiated a 202-day lockout of players, resulting in a loss of about $1 billion for owners and about half a billion dollars in foregone salaries for basketball players. Fans were frustrated and disenchanted, and supporters and advertisers lost millions. In 1999, the members of the World Trade Organization met in Seattle, Washington to lower trade barriers. The members of the organization could not even agree on an agenda and the meeting was an utter failure.

During 1999, Belinda Clark handled about 200 job offers for nursing assistants, research scientists, and a number of other employees. All but about 10 of these candidates took the initial offer without attempting to negotiate for something extra or more. Clark was delighted, but puzzled. The job applicants apparently did not realize that the offers Clark made were just starting points. She says, laughing, "I don't say anything if they don't." (Clark 1999, 88)

These examples suggest that negotiating is not easy. This is a problem, considering that people negotiate in their personal and business relationships, within organizations, between companies, across industries, and among nations.

Furthermore, negotiations occur between two people and, in other cases—such as the World Trade Organization—hundreds of people. The variety of negotiation contexts presents special challenges for managers, who are required to demonstrate competencies in all of these contexts. This book is designed to improve managers' and executives' negotiation skills across a wide variety of situations.

The working definition of *negotiation* used in this book is "an interpersonal decision-making process by which two or more people agree how to allocate scarce resources." By this definition, it is difficult to imagine how people can get through a single day without negotiating.

Negotiation as a Core Management Competency

Effective negotiation skills are increasingly important for executives, leaders, and managers in the business world. There are five key reasons for this.

Dynamic Nature of Business

Mobility and flexibility are the dictates of the new world of work. The dynamic, changing nature of business means that people must negotiate and renegotiate their existence in organizations throughout the duration of their careers. The advent of decentralized business structures and the absence of hierarchical decision-making provide opportunities for managers, but they also pose some daunting challenges. For example, most people do not stay in the same job that they take upon graduating from college or receiving their MBA degree; furthermore, most people will not have the same job as their predecessor. These realities mean that people must continually create possibilities, integrate their interests with others, and recognize that there will be competition both within companies and between companies (see Sidebar 1-1). Managers must be in a near-constant mode of negotiating opportunities.

Sidebar 1–1. New Businesses and Careers

According to *Business Week* (Alderman, 1999), it is the "era of the employee," with the tightest labour market in 29 years. This means that employees are in a one-up position, and employers need to keep them happy. For example, Doug Ross, the owner of Evolution Film & Tape Inc., a television production company in North Hollywood, California, lets his employees create their own hours, dress as they please, and bring their children to work—all in order to stay competitive. Employees and companies are in positions to negotiate all kinds of things, such as opportunities for training, flex time, family leave, health insurance, and other benefits. Another example: The California based Cheesecake Factory, Inc., pays salaries 20 percent above market rates. It also gives stock options to all its general managers, as well as new BMW 323s. This sounds expensive, but Cheesecake Factory says it has actually saved money, losing only two general managers in the last two years in an industry where a 38 percent turnover is the average (Conlin, Coy, Palmer, and Saveri 1999).

According to Linda Greene, associate vice-chancellor for academic affairs at the University of Wisconsin—Madison, "Many important events essential to professional success and professional satisfaction happen every day in the workplace and they are not always announced in advance" (Kalk 2000, 1E). In truth, negotiation comes into play when people participate in important meetings, get new assignments, head a team, participate in a reorganization process, and set priorities for their work unit (Kalk 2000). Ideally, negotiation should be second nature, but often, it is not.

Interdependence

The increasing interdependence of people within organizations, both laterally and hierarchically, implies that people need to know how to integrate their interests and work together across business units and functional areas. This not only occurs within companies, as people from different departments and units integrate their knowledge to create a product or service, but it also occurs between people from different companies, as is the case with strategic alliances. The increasing degree of specialization and expertise in the business world implies that people are more and more dependent on others to supply the components for a complete service or product. It is unwise to assume that others have similar incentive structures, so managers need to know how to promote their own interests while simultaneously creating joint value for their organizations. This requires negotiation.

Competition

Business is increasingly competitive. In today's economy, a few large firms are emerging as dominant players in the biggest markets. These industry leaders often enjoy vast economies of scale and earn tremendous profits. The losers are often left with little in the way of a market, let alone a marketable product (Frank and Cook 1995). This means that companies must be experts in the vast fields of competition. Managers not only need to function as advocates for their products and services, but they must also recognize the competition that is inevitable between companies and, in some cases, between units within a given company. Understanding how to navigate this competitive environment is essential for successful negotiation.

Information Age

The information age also provides special opportunities and challenges for the manager as negotiator. Computer technology, for example, extends a company's obligations and capacity to add value to its customers. This must be accomplished in a way that also benefits the company. Further, with ever-improving technology making it possible to communicate with people anywhere in the world, managers need to be able to negotiate at a moment's notice. Thus, the ability to determine relevant information from irrelevant information is critical for successful negotiation in the information overload age.

Diversity

Increasing diversity means that managers need to develop negotiation skills that can be successfully employed with people of different nationalities, backgrounds, and styles of communication. Thus, negotiators who have developed a bargaining style that works only within a narrow subset of the business world will suffer unless they can broaden their negotiation skills to effectively work with different people across functional units, industries, and cultures (Bazerman and Neale 1992). It is a challenge to develop a negotiation skill set generalizable enough to be used across different contexts, groups, and continents, but specialized enough to provide meaningful behavioural strategies in any given situation. This book provides the manager with such skills.

Most People are Ineffective Negotiators

Because negotiation is so important for personal and business success, it is rather surprising that most people do not negotiate very well—judging from their performance in realistic business negotiation simulations (for reviews, see Neale and Bazerman 1991; Thompson and Hrebec 1996; Thompson 1990a). For example, in a recent investigation of senior-level executives from major companies across the world, 95 per cent reached suboptimal outcomes in a realistic business simulation; in practical terms, they "left money on the table." They are not alone. A voluminous body of evidence indicates that people consistently leave money on the table; walk away from profitable deals and in some cases, settle for something worse than they could otherwise obtain by pursuing a different course of action.

The Major Sins of Negotiation

There are four major shortcomings in negotiation we have observed and documented in our research. They are:

1. *Leaving money on the table* (also known as "lose-lose" negotiation) occurs when negotiators fail to recognize and exploit win-win potential.

2. *Settling for too little* (also known as "the winner's curse") occurs when negotiators make too-large concessions, resulting in a too-small share of the bargaining pie.

3. *Walking away from the table* occurs when negotiators reject terms offered by the other party that are demonstrably better than any other option available to them. (Sometimes this is traceable to hubris or overweening pride; other times, it results from gross miscalculation.)

4. *Settling for terms that are worse than your alternative* (also known as the "agreement bias") occurs when negotiators feel obligated to reach agreement even when the settlement terms are not as good as their other alternatives.

This book teaches you how to avoid these errors, create value in negotiation, get your share of the bargaining pie, reach agreement when it is profitable to do so, and quickly recognize when agreement is not a viable option in a negotiation.

Why are People Ineffective Negotiators?

The dramatic instances of lose-lose outcomes, the winner's curse, walking away from the table, and the agreement bias raise the question of why people are not more effective at the bargaining table if negotiation is indeed critical for business success. The reason is not due to a lack of motivation or lack of intelligence on the part of negotiators. Many of the managers who fall victim to the major sins of negotiation do so for three primary causes: absence of feedback, satisfying, and self-reinforcement.

Absence of Relevant and Diagnostic Feedback

Most people have little opportunity to learn how to negotiate effectively. The problem is not lack of experience but a shortage of timely and accurate feedback. Even those people who have daily experiences in negotiation receive very little feedback on their negotiating effectiveness. The absence of feedback results in two human biases that further prevent negotiators from optimally benefiting from experience. The first problem is the *confirmation bias,* or the tendency for people to see what they want to see when appraising their own performance. The confirmation bias leads person to selectively seek information that confirms what they believe is true. Whereas the confirmation bias may seem perfectly harmless, it results in a myopic view of reality and can hinder learning. A second problem associated with the absence of relevant and diagnostic feedback is *egocentrism,* which is the tendency for people to view their experiences in a way that is flattering or fulfilling for them. This may increase a manager's self-esteem; however, in the long-run, it does a disservice to managers by preventing them from learning effectively. For example, it was egocentrism and the corresponding inability to recognize her own shortcomings that lead to the removal of Jill Barad as chairperson/CEO of toy maker Mattel Inc. (Byrne and Grover 2000). According to analysts, Barad never assumed responsibility for earnings surprises or adverse announcements. Instead, she blamed her subordinates and sacked them.

Satisficing

The second reason why people often fall short in negotiation is due to the human tendency to satisfied (Simon 1955). *Satisfying* is the opposite of *optimizing:* In a negotiation situation, as we will argue later in this book, it is important to optimize one's strategies by setting high aspirations and attempting to achieve as much as possible; in contrast, when people satisfied, they settle for something less than they could otherwise have. Over the long-run, satisfying (or the acceptance of mediocrity) can do one's self and one's company a disservice because there is a variety of effective negotiation strategies and skills that can be cheaply employed to result in dramatic increases in profit (we will discuss these strategies in detail in the next three chapters).

Self-reinforcement

The final reason why people perform poorly in negotiation is due to a principle known as *self-reinforcement,* which is the reluctance to try something new or change certain behaviours. It works like this: People are reluctant to change their behaviour and experiment with new courses of action because of the risks associated with experimentation. In short, the fear of losing keeps people from experimenting with change. Negotiators instead rationalize their behaviour in a self-perpetuating fashion. The fear of making mistakes may result in a manager's inability to improve his or her negotiation skills. In this book, we remove the risk of experimentation by providing several exercises and clear demonstrations of how changing one's behaviour can lead to better results in negotiation.

Debunking Negotiation Myths

Before we start on our journey toward developing a more effective negotiation strategy, we need to dispel several faulty assumptions and myths about negotiation. These myths hamper people's ability to learn effective negotiation skills and, in some cases, reinforce poor negotiation skills. In the following section, we expose the four most prevalent myths about negotiation behaviour.

Myth 1: Good Negotiators are Born

A pervasive belief is that good negotiation skills are something that people are born with, not something that can be readily learned. This is false because most excellent negotiators are self-made. In fact, there are very few naturally gifted negotiators. We tend to hear their stories, but we must remember that their stories are *selective,* meaning that it is always possible for someone to have a lucky day or a fortunate experience.

This myth is often perpetuated by the tendency of people to judge negotiation skills by their car-dealership experiences. Whereas purchasing a car is certainly an important and common type of negotiation, it is not the best context by which to judge your negotiation skills. The most important negotiations are those that we engage in every day with our colleagues, supervisors, co-workers, and business associates. These relationships provide a much better index of one's effectiveness in negotiation. In short, effective negotiation requires practice and feedback. The problem is that most of us do not get an opportunity to develop effective negotiation skills in a disciplined fashion; rather, most of us learn by doing. As the second myth reveals, experience is helpful, but not sufficient.

Myth 2: Experience is A Great Teacher

We have all met that person at the cocktail party or on the airplane who boasts about his or her great negotiation feats and how he or she learned on the job (Bazerman and Neale 1992). It is only partly true that experience can improve negotiation skills; in fact, naïve experience is largely ineffective in improving negotiation skills (Thompson and DeHarpport 1994). There are three strikes against natural experience as an effective teacher. First, in the absence of feedback, it is nearly impossible to improve performance.

For example, can you imagine trying to learn mathematics without ever doing homework or taking tests? Without diagnostic feedback, it is very difficult to learn from experience. The second problem is that our memories tend to be selective, meaning that people tend to remember their successes and forget their failures or shortcomings. This is, of course, comforting to our ego, but it does not improve our ability to negotiate. Finally, experience improves our confidence, but not necessarily our accuracy. People with more experience grow more and more confident, but the accuracy of their judgment and the effectiveness of their behaviour do not increase in a commensurate fashion. Overconfidence can be dangerous because it may lead people to take unwise risks.

Myth 3: Good Negotiators Take Risks

A pervasive myth is that effective negotiation necessitates taking risks and gambles. In negotiation, this may mean saying things like "This is my final offer" or "Take it or leave it" or using threats and bluffs. This is what we call a "tough" style of negotiation. Tough negotiators are rarely effective; however, we tend to be impressed by the tough negotiator. In this book, we teach negotiators how to evaluate risk, how to determine the appropriate time to make a final offer and, more importantly, how to make excellent decisions in the face of the uncertainty of negotiation.

Myth 4: Good Negotiators Rely on Intuition

An interesting exercise is to ask managers and anyone else who negotiates, to describe their approach to negotiating. Many seasoned negotiators believe that their negotiation style involves a lot of "gut feeling," intuition, and "in-the-moment" responses. We believe that this type of intuition does not serve people well. Effective negotiation involves deliberate thought and preparation and is quite systematic. The goal of this book is to help managers effectively prepare for negotiation, become more self-aware of their own strengths and shortcomings, and develop strategies that are *proactive* (*i.e.*, those that anticipate the reactions of their opponent) rather than *reactive* (*i.e.*, those that are dependent upon the actions and reactions of their opponent). Thus, excellent negotiators do not rely on intuition; rather, they are deliberate planners.

Learning Objectives

This book promises three things: First (and most important), reading this book will *improve your ability to successfully negotiate*. You and your company will be richer, and you will experience fewer sleepless nights, because you will have a solid framework and excellent toolbox for successful negotiation. However, in making this promise, we must also issue a warning: Successful negotiation skills do not come through passive learning. Rather, you will need to actively challenge yourself. We can think of no better way of doing this than to supplement this book with classroom experiences in negotiation, where managers can test their negotiation skills, receive timely feedback, and refine their negotiation strategies on a repeated basis.

Second, we provide you with a *general strategy for successful negotiation.* This book explicitly does not support a contextual model of negotiation, which prescribes using different negotiation strategies with different types of people, situations, and industries. Rather, we believe that negotiation skills are transferable across situations.

In saying this, we do not mean to imply that all negotiation situations are identical. This is patently false because negotiation situations differ dramatically across cultures and activities. However, there are key negotiation principles that are essential in all of these different contexts. The skills in this book are effective across a wide range of situations, ranging from complex, multiparty, multicultural deals to one-on-one personal exchanges.

Finally, this book offers an *enlightened model of negotiation.* Being a successful negotiator does not depend on your opponent's lack of familiarity with a book like this or a lack of training in negotiation. In fact, it would be ideal for you if your key clients and customers knew about these strategies. This approach follows what we call a *fraternal twin model,* which assumes that the other person you are negotiating with is every bit as motivated, intelligent, and prepared as you are. Thus, the negotiating strategies and techniques outlined in this book do not rely on "outsmarting" or tricking the other party; rather, they teach you to focus on simultaneously expanding the pie of resources and ensuring the resources are allocated in a manner that is favourable to you.

The Mind and Heart

Across all of the sections of this book, we focus on the *mind* of the negotiator as it involves the development of deliberate, rational, thoughtful strategies for negotiation. We also focus on the *heart* of the negotiator because it involves emotions, psychology, and the intuitive aspects of negotiation. This book strikes a balance between these two approaches to negotiation situations.

CHAPTER 9

Interpersonal Negotiation Skills

"Deep conflict requires a tremendous exertion of psychological and physical energy. ... Such conflict may be creatively transformed when adversaries come to learn, ironically perhaps, that they may fulfil their deepest needs and aspirations only with the co-operation of those who most vigorously oppose them." As we saw in Chapter 13, while discussing deep-seated interpersonal conflict, people are more willing to listen when they feel that they have been heard and have a sense of control over the outcome. In more traditional (or competitive) negotiations, instead, people often attempt to convince the other side of the merit or justice of their proposal. "If the other side understands our ideas," we reason, "surely they will agree with us." Merit and justice still play a role in interest-based negotiation, but so does exploring for solutions that meet mutual needs. Not everyone finds the interest-based concept easy to swallow, however, "Traditional negotiation techniques suggest you hide your true business needs and goals...," explains a grape grower who looks at the idea of interest-based negotiation with a certain amount of distrust. "Once the other side gets a hold of your real needs they will strangle you with that knowledge."

A little caution, if not cynicism, may well be necessary to survive. While we can attempt to model effective negotiation strategies when dealing with others, at times we may have to resort to a more traditional approach. Research has demonstrated, for instance, that those who are willing to "play to win," if so forced, yet prefer to attempt a mutually productive approach, may be more credible negotiators. Daniela, a young employee in one corporation, had heard of the difficult reputation developed by John, one of the agricultural technicians, but she had never had any difficulties with this individual herself. Daniela approached John one day, and found him sitting with his feet up on a table, reading a magazine. She apologized for disturbing him, assuming that perhaps this might have been his break period. "John, when you can, could you please pick up some parts for me in town?" Daniela asked politely. John answered rather curtly, "Right now?" She was not going to be intimidated, and responded, "That will work great for me, thanks!" John continued to show difficult behaviours with other individuals, but from then on never showed Daniela any discourtesy. I am not suggesting that Daniela took the very best approach available, but it served her well on that occasion.

The catch is that once people get caught up in competitive negotiation, it is often hard to step back and see clearly enough to work through difficulties in a collegial manner. A third person to help mediate may be needed (see Chapter 13). Traditional negotiation approaches have sometimes been described as including competition, yielding, withdrawal, or compromise. No one approach is always right or wrong. Competing means one person gets his way. Or at least it seems so at first. In the long-run both parties often end up losing. It does little good, for instance, to get a wonderful contract for your new swine facility, if the contractor is left with such a small profit margin that she goes out of business before completing it.

At one dairy, the incentive was to get done quickly. Employees were paid for the full shift even if they got done early. As one milker was washing his boots and preparing to go home, his supervisor asked if he could work into the next shift. When the milker got his paycheck, he was not given credit for the free time he had accumulated (as a result of quickly finishing his first shift). No amount of arguing helped convince his supervisor of how unfair this seemed. The milker refused any overtime work in the future. This is a perfect example of a win-lose outcome turning into a lose-lose scenario. Competition tends to focus on a particular episode, rather than on long-term viability; on the present goal rather than on the long-term relationship. I know a retired manager who brags that his subordinates soon learned "he was not always right—but always *the boss*." Although this manager may have obtained worker compliance from his winning tactics, I doubt he got much in terms of employee commitment. Losers often hold grudges, and find ways of getting even.

Should not a farmer try to obtain a good price for her apricot crop? Or get the best possible deal when buying that new piece of farm machinery? What about one-time situations, where you will never see another again in your life? Hidden in these questions, I believe there are some deeper issues that we must answer for ourselves. Surely, there *are* times when we bargain with the idea of getting the best possible results. In some cultures, people are offended if you pay the asking price without bargaining. But I will say this, many times in life we think we are dealing with a one-time situation, only to find that we have to negotiate or interact with that individual again.

Yielding (unilateral concessions at the expense of the person doing the giving in). We are most likely to yield if we feel there is little chance of winning, or if the outcome is more important to the other person than to us. "An angry co-worker began to shout and push me trying to pick a fight, and I left," a dairy worker explained. "For some reason I let it go and just backed away and left." The milker reflected that in his more youthful times he was a hot head, and would have probably fought back. Instead, when the dairy farmer returned, the worker reported the abusive incident to the dairyman, who fired the co-worker. In some situations yielding can be a virtue, but not always. A person who continues to yield sometimes stops caring. I do not see any harm in the occasional business yielding, or a balanced yielding among spouses, or even the frequent yielding obedience of a child to a parent or teacher. There are two specific types of yielding that concern me: (1) if saying yes today means living with frustration or resentment tomorrow, yielding is not a virtue; and related to that, (2) when we repeatedly agree to go along with a weak solution, this is not appropriate yielding, either (*e.g.*, because we want to avoid disagreement at all costs, or feel coerced). When we stop caring, we often withdraw physically or emotionally.

Compromise (mutual concessions where both parties yield some). Some types of compromises involve an arrangement somewhere between two positions; others may mean alternating the beneficiary. An example of the former is paying 20 cents per vine pruned when management wanted to pay 18 cents and crew workers asked for a quarter. An instance of the latter may involve alternating who gets to use the computer when there is limited computer time. While some issues lend themselves well to compromise, many others really do not. Compromise takes a measure of goodwill, trust and maturity, but not much creativity. But why is it that finding a middle ground can provide so little long-term satisfaction? Compromise often involves lazy communication and problem solving. For many of us, the term compromise certainly has come to have a negative connotation. While mutual concessions may take place at any time in the negotiation process, all too often such compromising occurs before the challenge has been sufficiently understood, or more creative solutions considered.

Our human brain is incredibly capable, when it comes to taking a huge amount of data and quickly digesting it and coming up with the one best solution. This is good, when it comes to making quick decisions in emergencies, and under time pressures. Unfortunately, making quick decisions can often deprive us of arriving at more effective, long lasting determinations. We are often too ready to accept a solution that seems to work, rather than the truly creative solution. The latter provides a sort of exhilaration. It is contagious. Once employees are involved to this degree, it is hard to turn back. You may have heard the classic tale of two siblings who argued over who would get an orange. They compromised and split it in half. One ate half and threw away the peel; the other, who was involved in a cooking project, grated the peel and discarded the rest. Compromise is good, especially when one considers the alternative, but creative or interest-based negotiation can provide much greater satisfaction.

Scenario 1: We want a raise Seven tractor drivers walked into a farm manager's office. These men had worked for the farm enterprise for several years. "We are all here," one of them began, slowly gathering confidence as he spoke. "Because we want a raise." The farm manager, somewhat stunned, turned around to look at each of them in unbelief. "How dare these guys come here, all together, and try and intimidate me into giving them a raise," he thought, but no words came out of his mouth. Two of the tractor drivers did most of the talking, and insisted that the manager either give them a raise, or they would quit.

So, what happened? The manager called the tractor drivers on their bravado or bluff, or so he thought. Soon he found himself without a single equipment operator as they had all quit in masse. The farm foreman in that operation tells us that when he went to town to purchase some parts a few hours later, he saw one of the tractor drivers walking aimlessly through town. The worker explained that he had no idea how he would face his wife. How he would tell her he had lost a job he had held for over five years. The foreman acted quickly, and the situation was somewhat salvaged, as the farm manager was able to convince four of the tractor drivers to come back and work for him.

Scenario 2: Leading by example? A foreman forced his will on the crew, but did it for a good cause. "No harm," he thought, "I am just trying to maximize all of our efforts." One day the crew workers were hungry and wanted to stop for lunch. The foreman wanted to get just a little more work done before lunch, and kept them going for another hour before breaking to eat. He could tell that a few workers were mumbling a bit, but he thought, "I am hungry too, I can wait for another hour, so can they."

So, what happened? "We were all very upset about this," one of the crew workers explained, speaking of the resentment felt at not being able to stop for lunch at the appointed hour. "The next time the foreman tried to make us work past lunch time we all walked off and left him fuming. The foreman told us to never do that to him again, but from then on he respected our need to stop at noon."

How have these farm operations been affected? What challenges do you think they may face in the future? How did the idea of "saving face" enter each of these situations? Even though some of the tractor drivers came back to work for the grower, do you think they will stay with him, or will they be looking for other work? Is there anything the farm manager could do now to improve the situation with the tractor drivers? How about the foreman, what can he do to recover the respect that has been lost?

What makes for an effective negotiator? Trustworthiness, for one, plays a huge role in successful negotiation. Dependability, honesty, and consistency are all part of trustworthiness. I often hear individuals involved in negotiations say, "I don't trust that person." It has also been said, "It is more important to be trusted than to be loved." As we break down negotiation talent into more specific type of skills, we can see that trust plays a large role in many, if not all of them. When we lose trust for a person, we begin to discount them. In our mind they begin to become undependable and dishonest. Some of the remaining scenarios will be broken down into multiple parts before the final resolution is given. Consider each of these parts fully in terms of what you would do, before reading what happened next. Some scenarios do not have a follow up, and leave you with the issue to reflect upon.

Scenario 3: Housing arrangements *Part I.* A horse breeder was facing some stress related to an employee living in a ranch-provided home. Actually, *not living* in the home would be a better description. The employee's wife had kicked him out a few weeks ago, and he was now sleeping in his pickup. It was important for the horse breeder to get his employee back in the house. They would soon be leaving for an important equestrian competition, and he just did not want to leave the issue up in the air.

So, what happened? Part II. The first step the horse breeder took was to find out if there was anything he could do to help repair the marriage difficulties. He offered to pay for marriage counseling. The wife was surprised and grateful that the farmer cared enough and agreed to let him know the next day. When the next day arrived, she informed the horse breeder that she had opted against counseling, and had made up her mind that she was leaving her husband. While the horse breeder did not want to sound crass, he did want to know when she would vacate the home.

So, what happened? *Part III.* The breeder knew that if the worker's wife pushed the issue, she could stay in the housing for quite a while. After talking a bit, the opportunity was right, and so he asked, trying not to seem overly anxious, "What are your plans?" She explained that she would need to stay in this home for at least one month, "We need to get together some money for a rental, including one month's deposit."

So, what happened? *Resolution*. The horse breeder first researched the cost of rental housing. When he approached the woman again, he was well prepared. "I realize it will be hard, but if you can manage to leave in two weeks, I will pay for one month's rental up to $X," he explained. "I realize it will be even harder, but if you manage to vacate the home in only one week, I will pay for two month's rental for you, or up to $2X." She was out in three days, after the horse breeder agreed to give her the cash instead of the rental payment. How may this horse breeding farm scenario have changed if the farmer would have made the same bottom line offer to help with the rental, but would have inverted the sentences so that the offer for leaving in one week would have been brought up first? "I realize it will be hard, but if you manage to vacate the home in one week, I will pay for two month's rental for you, up to $2X. If you leave in two weeks, however, I will pay for one month's rental up to $X."

Prepare

To prepare effectively, one needs to know as much as possible about all aspects of the situation and the personalities involved. Cost comparisons are essential when dealing with economic issues. There has been much written about being a smart shopper. Sometimes the most unexpected issues may come up. You may, for instance, have to face a worker who has come asking for a loan to bury a family member. One worker was struck by the tragedy of his young wife's untimely death. He was going to have to pay $4,700 for the funeral (not including the graveside plot). With a little calling around, the farmer's wife discovered that the same service could be had for $1,024. Sure, the second funeral home was not providing caskets that were as fancy, or flowers. She figured that for those savings, they could purchase their own flowers.

Being prepared, may also mean better understanding the style of the person one will be dealing with. For instance, if you are exporting your fruit to Asia, and are meeting with prospective buyers, you may want to know as much as possible about the proper etiquette and preferences of your guests. Should you plan to get right to the point, for instance, or take more time talking about other pre-negotiation issues? Is there a right or a wrong way to handle greetings? Even details, such as how to accept a business card, may play an important role in showing the potential buyers the proper respect. In some Asian cultures, for instance, the proper etiquette is to hold the card with both hands and take time to study it carefully. You keep the card before you throughout the meeting, rather than putting it away in your wallet. An effective way to prepare for very difficult or emotionally charged situations is to role play ahead of time. Role playing the opposite perspective can be particularly enlightening.

Search for Clarity

As negotiators, it helps to learn about other people's preferences and also make our own clear. One grower explained that it was hard enough to understand our own needs and preferences, let alone be able to concentrate on someone else's. And perhaps that is one of the reasons why we do not see as frequent a use of interest-based negotiation. It does take a certain amount of effort, especially at first. With time, it can begin to feel more natural.

In the 1980s, when the non-smoking movement had not yet reached Chile, I taught a graduate course on labour management. Perhaps as many as 80 per cent of my students smoked. I was clearly in the minority. I did not want to be rude, but I also knew that tobacco smoke would give me a headache. "I want to encourage everyone who wishes to smoke, to do so whenever they wish," I began. "Nevertheless, I would ask that you just step outside the classroom to do so." This was taken positively, and several in the class even nodded their approval. Part of effective preparation is considering the worse possible scenario, or "best alternative to a negotiated agreement" (BATNA). I suppose that even not agreeing to negotiate is a form of negotiation. If we cannot come to an agreement, what is the worst possible outcome to this situation? If your neighbour has a dispute with you over water rights? If the only welding shop in town substantially raises their prices? If your son threatens to leave the dairy if you do not meet certain conditions?

Show Patience

Effective negotiation frequently calls for a great amount of patience. Logic is not the only thing that prevails in bargaining efforts. There is a lot that comes into play in the form of interpersonal relations. Allowing other people as well as ourselves the time to work out problems is essential. When dealing with someone of a dissimilar culture, we may also need to allot additional time to work out an agreement. Not coming across as *wanting something too much* is related to patience. When we become overly narrow as to the result we will accept, we put ourselves at a negotiation disadvantage. So it was when my wife and I bought our first home. We were so openly delighted with it, that we lost an opportunity to bargain much over price. Of course, there is a balance between being *desperate* and playing *hard to get*, neither of which is very positive.

Maintain Integrity

At a time when many decisions were made on a handshake, my parents invited all the children to a family conference. "Earlier this year," they explained, "we came to an agreement with the winery for a price. Since then, many vineyards were affected by a terrible freeze, one that has meant a huge decline in supply. Had we waited a few more months before coming to an agreement on the price for our wine, we could have gotten a much better deal." My parents asked each of their five children for their opinions. The answer was a unanimous agreement to honour the oral agreement. At the time, I felt impressed that my parents would ask for our input. Since then I have come to the conclusion that they knew the answer all along, but wanted to teach us an important lesson about integrity. It is really impossible to have a discussion about *trust* and neglect the issue of integrity. Integrity in business and in every part of our lives is completely tied to our ability to be effective negotiators and be considered trustworthy.

Avoid the Presumption of Evil

"And she didn't even sign the E-mail!" the farmer complained. He had a bitter taste as a result of some dealings with a local government agency. In a world of increasing electronic correspondence, the possibilities for misunderstanding are ever increasing. When using E-mail, there is much we can do to become better communicators ourselves. Nevertheless, it is dangerous to assume that someone did not sign so she could offend us. This is especially so when the person's name already appears as part of the E-mail address.

E-mail etiquette is no different than any other type of good manners. There is a great variation in what people consider polite. For instance, in some cultures it is considered good manners to leave the toilet seat down. In others, the polite thing is to leave it up so it can stay clean. In some Hispanic sub-cultures it is rude for a man to greet the wife of a friend with a kiss on the cheek; in others, it is rude not to. While we want to make every effort to be polite ourselves, it is best to avoid being judgmental about other people's behaviour. At one ranch operation, one of the partners tended to assume that the other two partners were talking about him when he saw them conversing. This is called negative attribution. It is all too easy to incorrectly interpret another person's innocent behaviour and assume the worst. Contention breeds mistrust. It is good *not to be easily provoked,* especially when no offense was intended.

Some years ago I was asked to give a talk to a group of young adults. I noticed that as I spoke, a young man would lean toward the young lady beside him and whisper. I found this to be very distracting. I feel very strongly that only one person should speak at a time, and so it was that every time he began to talk, I stopped. When I stopped, he stopped, and so it went. I later found out he was interpreting for a foreign visitor. On another occasion, I attended a meeting where my supervisor was pointing out some problems. I began to defend myself. "We were not talking about you," the supervisor said calmly. It is embarrassing to run at "the sound of a shaken leaf" when no one pursues. It is good to avoid assumptions, or to become defensive. An effective tool, instead of assuming the worse when we do not know how to interpret something, is to describe what happened and let the other person explain. Such a description should avoid inferences as to why someone did something. We will often find out there was a good reason for what took place. Or at least give each party the opportunity to explain her perspective.

Control Emotions

Our emotions get in the way of effective negotiations regularly. Nothing kills creativity quicker than anger, pride, embarrassment, envy, greed, or other strong negative emotion. Anger is often an expression of fear, or lack of confidence in our ability to get what we think we want. Emotional outbursts tend to escalate rather than solve a conflict. If we can improve our ability to manage our emotions and respond without getting defensive, we have gone a long way toward creative negotiation. A friend once said, "When we permit negative emotions, such as anger, to take control of us, this is a sure sign we are about to step into a trap."

It is extremely difficult to hide our emotions, especially when we feel there is much in the balance. Our body language, particularly our facial gestures and voice tonal qualities, often give us away. We are not emotionless robots, nor is it advantageous to completely hide our emotions. However, it is better to *describe* our emotions (*e.g.*, a feeling of disappointment) rather than to *show* them.

Scenario 4: I won't work for that foreman *Part I.* A peach grower hired a foreman who was very effective. The man was kind, but firm. Some of the equipment operators, accustomed to work without supervision, highly resented having a foreman. "We just do not want a foreman," some of the employees had told the grower. The farmer noticed that jobs that used to take much longer to accomplish were being completed in a much more timely fashion.

So, what happened? Part II. The grower wanted to make sure the foreman was respectful of the employees, was giving them their proper breaks, providing them with cold water, and doing all the things a thoughtful foreman should do. This seemed to be so in every way, but it had not been a week since the grower started to investigate the situation, when one of the most outspoken workers came to speak to him. Most of the other workers had adjusted to having a foreman, especially after the grower went out of his way to explain what the duties of the foreman would be, and how having a foreman would allow the grower to spend more time taking care of other orchard duties. The worker seemed agitated, and upset, and soon set out the ultimatum, "I will not work here with *this* foreman," he blurted out his feelings. So, what happened? *Part III.* Fifteen years ago this peach grower would have fired the crew worker for insubordination. Now, as he was getting older, the grower had mellowed out considerably. He knew the importance of listening to others. "What's the matter?" he inquired solicitously. "Well, its just not right," the crew worker responded, still upset. "The man does not have a foreman's license!"

So, what happened? *Part IV.* The grower wanted to laugh at this response. He had heard almost every story in the book during his years in farming, ever since he started working alongside his dad as a youngster. But this one was a new one. While the grower knew that there was much about the law he did not know, he was clear on this point. There was no law that required foremen to have a supervisor's license. But then, he looked at it from the worker's perspective, and realized that there really was not anything funny about the employee's concerns. "Did you know that here in California a foreman does not need a license?" he began. As far as the grower knew, there was no state that required a license, but he wanted to make sure that the employee did not lose face or feel foolish. "What you say is important, maybe foremen *should* be required to have a license, just like farm labour contractors," he added in an effort to further validate the employee. "Tell me, now that you know that a foreman's license is not required in California" the grower eventually asked, "how do you feel about working for me?" "I just don't know," the worker spoke now much more calmly, but was shaking his head somewhat. The grower tried to find out if there was something else that was the matter, but made no discovery that cleared up the situation.

So, what happened? *Part V.* The grower felt his own options narrowing, and was about to tell the crew worker that he was fired if he could not work for the foreman. Then he remembered that the worker had asked for additional time off for the Thanksgiving holiday weekend. It was now the day before Thanksgiving. The grower was amazed when he heard himself asking, "Would you like some time to think about it? You had asked for time off during the Thanksgiving weekend. Would Tuesday of next week work for you?" The crew worker agreed and seemed satisfied, and began to leave. "Wait a moment," the grower stopped him. "Do not forget to take the turkey I bought for you," he said cheerfully, pretending there was nothing wrong as he handed over the big bird. As he watched the worker disappear with the turkey, what amazed the grower the most about himself was that he had stayed calm through the whole situation, never getting angry at the employee. So, what happened? *Resolution.* The grower knew that despite his own calm, there was still something wrong. As he stood there watching the worker leave, the grower saw the employee put the turkey in a co-worker's pickup. The worker did not wait until Tuesday to come back and talk to the grower. Friday morning he showed up asking, "You do not have work for me?!" In reality, it sounded more like a statement rather than a question. "Actually, we *do* have work for you," the grower answered. "No, you do not understand," the worker continued apprehensively. "You do *not* have work for me!" "But we *do* have work for you," the grower repeated. Finally, the worker clarified, "You see, now I cannot collect Unemployment Insurance!" The worker had wanted to be fired, because those who quit are not eligible for Unemployment Insurance in California.

Understand Time Pressures

Deadlines are often self-imposed. How often do we feel obligated to respond right away when facing a difficult situation? People can ask for a little more time to study out a matter, or to accomplish a task. Do not be afraid to ask, "This is a tough one, can you give me until 3 p.m. tomorrow to get back to you?" Or, "It is now 7:15 a.m., and I am tied up for the next two hours. If I call you between 10 and 10:30 a.m., will that work for you?" This type of detail only takes a few minutes longer to negotiate. "I will call you back as soon as I can," on the other hand, leaves much to be desired. As a recipient of that message we may wonder, does that mean I will receive a call in the next half hour, two hours, or week? Although not intended as such, this may well come across as an avoidance tactic. To be credible, then, it is important to agree on a specific time wherein we will get back to a person. We also need to be specific about exactly what it is that we have agreed to accomplish.

If we can build a little cushion for the unexpected, that is helpful. Most people do not mind having to wait a little longer if they know what the real situation is. Armed with such knowledge, each individual can plan her own time more effectively, rather than wait for another person who may or may not come through. If a deadline seems hard to meet, ask to re-negotiate an extension *before* the time for the deadline is up. An effective negotiator will ask the other party to suggest or take a role in establishing a deadline, rather than arbitrarily impose one. Furthermore, it is good to give others the time they need to make a decision with which they are comfortable. To do what we say we will do, and do so in a timely fashion, builds trust. People who can be counted to follow through with what they say they will do are invaluable.

Break Down Bigger Issues into Smaller Ones

An effective negotiator is constantly looking for ways to break down challenges into smaller, more easily solvable issues. For instance, if a farm foreman is resisting the introduction of an electronic gadget to help keep track of each crew member's performance, it helps to talk it over, and find out specific concerns. There may be some apprehension about (1) the reliability of the system, (2) setup time, or even (3) staying on top of production data right in the field. Each of these concerns can be addressed separately.

Separate Problem from Self-worth

Without a doubt, the worst type of intermixing issues is that of combining some problem that is important to us with our own self-worth. It is ineffective and manipulative, for instance, to imply that disagreement with our idea is equivalent with a vote of no-confidence against us. Such an approach, will sooner than later result in our feeling reject.

A member of a dairy's corporate board (who also happened to be one of the founders of the original dairy), made the mistake of suggesting that a vote against the incentive pay programme she was suggesting for the milers was equivalent to a vote against her. After the meeting, she confronted a member of the board who voted against the proposal as it presently stood. She was fortunate that this individual was willing to stand up to such pressure. He explained that as long as he was a member of the board he would vote for what was best for the dairy. And furthermore, the board member told the founder that he did not appreciate being pushed into doing anything short of voting his conscience. The founder apologized.

Avoid Threats and Manipulative Tactics

Threats also reduce our negotiating ability. Such threats may entail a directed consequence – towards ourselves or someone else. Any type of threat can greatly undermine our long-term negotiating ability. This is even more so, when an individual does not follow through. Threats do not engender trust or liking. Even inconsequential threats can be annoying. At a family game, one player repeatedly threatened to quit. After a half dozen threats, his mother told him, "The first time you threatened, I was concerned, by the last threat, I was just ready for you to quit and let the rest of us enjoy the game." Sometimes we may not realize that sharing some of our discouragement may come across as a threat. My research shows that people in deep seated interpersonal organizational conflict, more often than not, are seriously contemplating bailing out the organization. Yet, these individuals have seldom told others at the farm that they are contemplating withdrawal. And that is good!

One farm manager who would continually threaten those around him with comments about leaving the farm operation, began to quickly lose the support of others around him. The respect that this individual so much wanted from his colleagues began to vanish, and even his loyalty to the organization was questioned. While people often feel a great need to share their feelings with someone who can be supportive, we need to choose such a person with care. If the individual always agrees with us and validates our perspective, such a person may not be doing us a favour. People who feel validated elsewhere may put less effort into improving a failing relationship. A positive relationship, is one where the listener can help us identify where we may have contributed to the problem. We all need people who can help us see the *blind spots* in our personalities and behaviors.

Focus on the Problem Rather than the Solution

The suggestion of focusing on the problem rather than the solution may sound counter intuitive. Yet for a number of reasons, it is one of the keys to effective negotiation. The more complex the situation, the more important this principle. When someone comes with the solution, even when that solution is a good one, it gives the other stakeholder the feeling of not having any control. Research has shown that people often prefer an outcome that is not as beneficial, yet one where they sense greater control over possible outcomes. Even if a stakeholder has gone out of his way to find a fair solution for all involved, when such a solution is presented as firm, it tends to put other stakeholders on the defensive. In one such case, a rancher who was presented with such a stance (i.e., given the solution) felt coerced to do all the compromising. What this stakeholder did not realize until later, is that the solution being presented was already a huge concession and compromise on the part of the other stakeholder who presented it. The timing and approach had been ineffective, however.

An individual with an excellent idea needs to wait until the predicament that has brought everyone together has been carefully discussed, and until the needs of all the stakeholders are understood. Only then can the solution be presented, and this needs to be done in a very tentative fashion. "Would such and such an idea meet your needs, or can we play with the concept and twist it a bit so it does?"

Where there is an emotionally charged atmosphere, or when there is much riding in terms of consequences for individual stakeholders, this approach may make a difference between success and failure. An effective negotiating technique, then, is to come to the bargaining table with the idea of studying the problem and individual needs, rather than imposing a solution. This approach of coming right out with a fair solution, but doing away with all the bargaining, is known to most of us as the "take it or leave it" tactic. In collective bargaining, it is called *Boulwarism*, named after former General Electric (GE) Vice President Lemuel R. Boulware. What management would do was to propose a final offer to the union right up front. Management went out of their way to study all the facts that could pertain to the contract, and to make it fair for all involved, "trying to do right voluntarily." They refused to budge from their position, however, unless any "new facts" of sufficient strength were presented. Such an approach was highly resented by the union, who felt undermined. Two "new facts" played key roles against Boulwarism, (1) the practice was found to some degree, to constitute bad-faith bargaining by the National Labor Relations Board (NLRB) and the courts; and (2) the union also made a very strong point against the tactic through a successful strike.

When we are the ones being presented with a possible solution, it is good to be slow to find fault. If someone's proposal is quickly followed by our counterproposal, the other individual is likely to feel slighted. Two key reasons for avoiding quick counterproposals include (1) the other stakeholder is least receptive to hear another proposal after setting hers on the table, and (2) such counteroffers are often perceived as disagreement, or an affront to "face."

At the very least, then, efforts should be made to let the other stakeholders feel that their proposal is being taken seriously, and has been understood. If a counterproposal builds on the other stakeholder's proposal, and credit is so given, then the chances for negative feelings are further curtailed.

Scenario 5: Poor quality pack A greenhouse manager has had terrible results this year in terms of tomatoes being picked outside of the acceptable color range. He asked both the assistant production manager and the foreman to work on the difficulty. The foreman insisted that the problem was caused by the incentive pay programme. In his opinion workers were paying little interest to quality issues, as there was no negative consequence for poor quality. The assistant manager, on the other hand, felt that a return to hourly pay would greatly reduce productivity. Plus, she remembers that last year, when workers were paid by the hour, they still had problems with quality.

Who are all the possible individuals that can be affected by this challenge? Do they have any common needs? What might these be? Are there some hidden challenges here? How could we be more sure that the correct problem was understood?

Try for Interest-based Solutions

In traditional negotiations (*i.e.,* focused on competition, yielding or compromise), we are inclined to focus exclusively on our needs and assume it is the other stakeholder's responsibility to worry about having her needs met. Yet, by showing a sincere interest in the needs of others we increase the chances of having our needs met. While talking about our needs may have been considered a selfish thing in traditional negotiation, here in creative negotiation it is not selfish by definition, as it is not only our needs that are being considered, but also the needs of the other stakeholders. We frequently fail to explore beyond the obvious solution—like the sisters who split the orange in half. It helps to validate the other stakeholder's needs as a starting point in exploring creative solutions and as a way to reduce negative emotion. "Hmm ... you need to get home by four today. Let's think of how we can do that and get the animals fed, too." Integrative negotiation seeks to carefully understand the true nature of the problem, and genuinely attempt, where it is possible, to provide solutions that meet the respective needs of all who are affected.

In recent years there have been some very positive developments in the field of negotiation, including union-management relations. The past has offered a frequently adversarial, turbulent and sometimes violent approach to collective bargaining and labour union-management relations. These positive changes, which have in no way been universally adopted, have come about as a result of an interest-based negotiation approach. Union representatives are becoming more conscious of the need to increase the competitiveness of unionized employers, while further enhancing job security and quality of life for all employees. Employers under a union contract are more likely to work with rather than against the union, to meet both worker and organizational needs. I have had the opportunity to watch representatives of union and management sitting side by side, and enthusiastically reporting success after success with the interest-based approach. At the very core of creative negotiation is the idea that it is possible for everyone to get more of what they need by working together. The foundation of effective problem-solving understands the problem itself. Otherwise, it is all too easy to build solutions on a false foundation. After such understanding, creative negotiation involves looking for the hidden opportunities presented by challenges.

Having said all this, it is not easy to be *creative*. It takes work. The following five-step process has been suggested to get the creative juices flowing: (1) actively consider all alternatives; (2) digest and re-arrange the data; and (3) set the challenge aside and wait. Wait for what? ... for a (4) sudden flash of inspiration, which needs to be; (5) rigorously tested. These steps are important, as they recognize the importance of looking at a challenge from all angles, studying out a problem, and then putting it aside for a time. I suspect that sometimes steps one through three may need to be repeated several times until that inspiration comes. As we practice creative negotiation, faith in our ability to turn challenges into opportunities will increase. This self-confidence will help us focus on problem solving and reduce the chances of falling back on contention, negative emotion or competitive negotiation.

Admit Error and Apologize

We mentioned earlier that strong negative emotion can lead us into psychological traps. So can over-investment in an idea. If the foundation is wrong, we may have to undo all our work and begin from scratch. Depending how far into a project we are, this can be quite painful and expensive. We have to first recognize that we *have been wrong* before we can *make things right.* If we notice that the concrete foundation to the dairy barn we are building is faulty, we can close our eyes and continue construction only at our own peril. As painful as it may seem now, the sooner we recognize our error and make the necessary expenditures to break up and remove the concrete so we can start over, the better off we are.

Sometimes we may feel over-invested in terms of an idea. It may be as hard to admit we were wrong as it was to break up that concrete. People who are willing to admit a mistake are more likely to be considered trustworthy. A proper apology is extremely powerful. So is sharing a goal we have in terms of a new approach to dealing with issues. If we have been extremely critical in the past, it helps to let people know we will be working to improve that negative pattern. To be genuine, an apology must not come across as a justification for what we have done wrong. A true apology is also accompanied with an offer to make restitution when that is possible. Furthermore, a sincere apology implies a willingness to make the appropriate changes commensurate with what we have done wrong. When I feel it is warranted, I like the idea of asking a person to whom I am apologizing, "Will you accept my apology?"

When someone expresses regret often for the same thing but makes no real efforts to change, this is hardly an apology. As powerful as an apology can be, when someone takes back that apology by word or deed, this puts such an individual in a position of greater disadvantage than if she had expressed no regrets at all. Such is the situation, for instance, in many cases of domestic violence (physical or verbal). It is not uncommon for a man to be contrite after beating his wife today. But by tomorrow he has begun to minimize the damage, and not long thereafter is striking her again. A person who is willing to accept an apology, and forgive another, is likewise in a better position than one who is not. It is also hard to trust a person who will not acknowledge an apology. An individual who has truly forgiven another does not continually remind the other of that fact. Some comments and deeds are so hurtful in their nature, however, that it may take extensive time before a person can truly feel free of the associated pain.

Reject Weak Solutions

In traditional negotiation, as soon as we get close enough to the solution we want, we are often prone to accept someone's yielding their will to ours. While at times the motivation on our part may be selfish, in others we may truly believe that our solution will best serve all involved. Then again, earlier we said that (1) it was difficult for true caring to co-exist with frequent giving in; and (2) jumping to solutions before the problem is carefully understood, often yields weak solutions. Sometimes people will yield or pretend to yield out of frustration over the situation. By accepting their yielding, we have reduced our direct and indirect negotiation power. Instead, we not only get better solutions when we make sure the other person is completely satisfied with the solution, but we gain trust in their eyes and can thus improve our negotiation strength.

Scenario 6: Disagreement over the radio Two milkers had a disagreement over which radio station to listen to. "I don't know," one of them sighed as he lifted his hands in disappointment, "just choose whichever station you want." So, what happened? *Resolution*. The one milker accepted the defeat of the other, and began to walk towards the radio. But before the milker arrived to where the radio was located at the other side of the parlor, his co-worker protested, "That's just not right, why should you get your way." Their negotiation process had to begin anew.

Sometimes people give in easily. We should not be quick to accept such yielding. Taking extra time to consider alternatives can be very rewarding. We may often sense that another person is giving in, rather than agreeing that the solution that has been suggested is indeed the best possible alternative. If you read emotion or strength of conviction in another stakeholder (or the very opposite), you may want to step back and consider together what unmet needs may exist still, and work towards finding a solution that takes these into consideration.

Sidebar 17-1: Not so fast! Benie and Jennifer Matsuda were making some joint succession plans for their farm operation. They came to an agreement, but Benie noticed that his wife had only agreed hesitantly. Rather than just accepting Jennifer's agreement and moving on with his own plans, Benie said, "I notice that you are not totally pleased with our decision. It is really important to me that this is right, and that you are as happy with this decision as I am."

Jennifer said she was OK with the decision, but Benie still sensed otherwise. Benie had the perfect opportunity to move forward and do things the way he wanted to, but hesitated again. "I still sense there is something you are feeling, perhaps difficult to put into words, but nevertheless something important that makes you hesitate." Jennifer answered, "Actually, I think you may be right." She agreed to think over the matter some more. That night they had another chance to converse at length, and Jennifer was able to better articulate a fear she had. As a result they were able to make some small but important adjustments that left them both satisfied. Moreover, Jennifer was able to further build her trust on her husband, because he had honoured her feelings, thoughts, and opinions.

Be Tentative about Reading People's Feelings

Attributions should be neutral or tentative, such as "I sense there is something wrong here." Avoid attributing negative emotions to another person, such as "You are angry." Nor should one ascribe a reason along an attribution, "You must be hurt because we switched to 3x milking." Instead, just describe the emotion in more neutral ways, and with some degree of tentativeness, allowing the other stakeholder to either validate these feelings, or offer their own explanation: "I sense that something is still not right in our agreement, but I am not sure if I am reading that correctly."

Summary

Each one of us negotiates our way through life. While there are no easy answers that will fit every negotiation need, there are some important principles that will help us become more effective. Creative negotiation skills at first seem different enough from how we may have reacted to challenges in the past that reading a chapter and a book such as this one, only begins to plant some ideas in our minds. Some of the approaches may seem mechanical at first. I like to keep these thoughts alive from day to day by reading good books, or listening to audio tapes. Furthermore, I tend to analyze human interaction. There is much to be learned from both interpersonal success and failure.

There are many excellent books available on the topics of negotiation skills, listening skills, conflict management, interpersonal communications, and so on. Try your local library and you may find some real treasures. After I read a book or listen to a tape, I like to note the most important things I have learned from each. You may want to do the same, keeping special notes on the outcomes of your negotiations. As I grow older, *doing right* has become more important to me than *being right* (in the sense of winning). There is a great amount of satisfaction in being able to give the *soft answer* ("A soft answer turneth away wrath"). This is a journey that one embarks in, the challenge of which is so difficult, that one can never truly say, "I have arrived there." May your own excursion be filled with satisfaction and hope.

A Final Note

Your comments about this book will be greatly welcomed. I wish you prosperity in your farming enterprise and success in the management of people on your farm. I invite you to explore our Website and join the AG-HRnet or to receive our electronic newsletter People in Ag. If you have any comments, suggestions, or questions, please feel free to contact me.

The very thought of negotiating sounds intimidating, yet we are all experienced negotiators. Any time we come to an agreement on anything, we are negotiating. Some of it we may do somewhat subconsciously, such as deciding who says hello first, or holding a cattle gate open for another rider to pass through. Determining where to go out for dinner with your spouse, or asking your daughter for help in training a colt also involves negotiation. More traditional issues we associate with negotiation may include agreeing on (1) a pruning price with your vineyard crew; (2) how much you are going to pay to have your post-harvest cooling shed constructed; or (3) what you will get for your export cherries. One thing that these examples have in common, is that they involve people. Many of us developed a love for agriculture based on our love for farm animals and plants. We may at first be surprised to see instead, what a large portion of our day involves interacting with people. Although negotiation can be downright hard at times, there are specific steps we can take to become more effective negotiators.

Negotiation skills include being well prepared, showing patience, maintaining integrity, avoiding the presumption of evil, controlling our emotions, understanding the role of time pressures, breaking down bigger issues into smaller ones, avoiding threats and manipulative tactics, focusing first on the problem rather than on the solution, seeking for interest-based decisions, and rejecting weak solutions. We shall visit these later on in the chapter. A fair portion of this book incorporates negotiation principles in one way or another. This chapter is presented as a way to help us think through challenging day-to-day situations, especially those for whom we may not find direct answers in the book. I find that it helps to keep a mental or written notebook on how we react to difficult situations. Certainly, we have lots of opportunities to practice. While still focusing on agricultural labour management, it is my hope in this chapter to expand to other *people issues* that affect us. Whatever improvements we make in one area of our lives, these tend to spill over to other areas, such as the home, ranch, business dealings, or sports. For those of you who operate a family farm, many such distinctions are already blurry.

Interspersed through this chapter, a number of scenarios are provided for you to practice negotiation skills. Set aside your reading after each one, and think through all the issues that may be involved. How do you think you would react to each case? Put yourself in the place of each of the players. Only after considering each scenario separately, move on to find out how they were resolved. While resolutions are provided for most scenarios, please note that these may *not* reflect the best or worst possible outcome. Furthermore, what is *best* for one stakeholder may not be for the other. You may want to ask yourself, in what ways could these individuals have arrived at a better solution. Finally, the scenarios are placed somewhat randomly throughout the chapter, and are not necessarily intended to reflect the topic discussed in that section.

REFERENCES

1. Rothman, J. (1997). *Resolving Identity-Based Conflict in Nations, Organizations, and Communities* (pp. xii, xiii). San Francisco: Jossey-Bass Publishers.
2. Fisher, R., & Ury, W. (1981). *Getting to Yes: Negotiating Agreement Without Giving In*. New York, NY: Penguin Books.
3. Alavi, K. Personal conversations.
4. Swann, W. B., Jr. (1996). *Self-Traps: The Elusive Quest for Higher Self-Esteem* (p. 47). New York: W. H. Freeman and Company.

5. Sloane, A. A., & Witney, F. *Labour Relations* (4th Edition) (pp. 205-206). Englewood Cliffs, New Jersery: Prentice-Hall Inc.; and Peterson, W. (April 1991). "Ideas Have Consequences." Commencement Address to Harvard Business School Alumni. *The Freeman*, a publication of the Foundation for Economic Education, Inc., (Vol. 41, No. 4) in "Liberty Haven" Website.
6. Rackham, N. (1999). "The Behaviour of Successful Negotiators," in Lewicki *et. al.* (Editors). *Negotiation: Readings, Exercises, and Cases* (3rd Edition) (p. 347). Burr Ridge, Illinois: Irwin.
7. Sperber, P. (1983). *Fail-Safe Business Negotiating* (pp. 10-21). Englewood Cliffs, N. J.: Prentice Hall, in Lewicki *et. al.* (Editors); *Negotiation: Readings, Exercises, and Cases* (1993) (2nd Edition) (p. 173). Burr Ridge, Illinois: Irwin.

Managerial Negotiations

Negotiating is the process of communicating back and forth, for the purpose of reaching a joint agreement about differing needs or ideas. It is a collection of behaviours that involves communication, sales, marketing, psychology, sociology, assertiveness and conflict resolution. A negotiator may be a buyer or seller, a customer or supplier, a boss or employee, a business partner, a diplomat or a civil servant. On a more personal level negotiation takes place between spouse's friends, parents or children.

It is a process of interaction by which two or more parties who consider that they need to be jointly involved in an outcome, but who initially have different objectives, seek by the use of argument and persuasion to resolve their difference in order to achieve a mutually acceptable solution. Another important consideration is that negotiation implies acceptance by both parties that agreement between them is required before a decision can be implemented.

The art of negotiation is based on attempting to reconcile what constitutes a good result for the other party. To achieve a situation where both sides win something for themselves, you need to be well prepared, alert and flexible. There are seven basic principles common to all forms of negotiation:

- There are minimum two parties involved in the negotiation process. There exists some common interest, either in the subject matter of the negotiation or in the negotiating context that puts or keeps the parties in contact.
- Though the parties have the same degree of interest, they initially start with different opinions and objectives which hinders the outcome in general.
- In the beginning, parties consider that negotiation is a better way of trying to solve their differences.
- Each party is under an impression that there is a possibility of persuading the other party to modify their original position, as initially parties feel that they shall maintain their opening position and pursuade the other to change.
- During the process, the ideal outcome proves unattainable but parties retain their hope of an acceptable final agreement.
- Each party has some influence or power—real or assumed—over the other's ability to act.
- The process of negotiation is that of interaction between people-usually this is direct and verbal interchange.

Negotiation is a skill that anyone can learn and practice. The necessary skills required for successful negotiations can be listed as :

- The ability to define a range of objectives, yet be flexible about some of them.
- The ability to explore the possibilities of a wide range of options.

- The ability to be well prepared.
- The ability to listen to and question other parties.
- The ability to set priorities.

These are useful abilities, not only in negotiations but in daily life as well. It is useful to remember that the ability to influence and persuade is one of the most essential of all management skill—and influence and persuasion are very much the stuff of effective negotiation.

Depending upon the situation and time, the way the negotiations are to be conducted differs. The skills of negotiations depends and differs widely from one situation to the other. Basically the types can be divided into three broad categories.

Types	Parties Involved	Examples
Day-to-day/ Managerial Negotiations	1. Different levels of Management 2. In between colleagues 3. Trade unions 4. Legal advisers	1. Negotiation for pay, terms and working conditions. 2. Description of the job and fixation of responsibility. 3. Increasing productivity.
Commercial Negotiations	1. Management 2. Suppliers 3. Government 4. Customers 5. Trade unions 6. Legal advisors 7. Public	1. Striking a contract with the customer. 2. Negotiations for the price and quality of goods to be purchased. 3. Negotiations with financial institutions as regarding the availability of capital.
Legal Negotiations	1. Government 2. Management 3. Customers	1. Adhereing to the laws of the local and national government.

1. Day-to-day/Managerial Negotiations: Such types of negotiations are done within the organization and are related to the internal problems in the organization. It is in regards to the working relationship between the groups of employees. Usually, the manager needs to interact with the members at different levels in the organization structure. For conducting the day-to-day business, internally, the superior needs to allot job responsibilities, maintain a flow of information, direct the record keeping and many more activities for smooth functioning. All this requires entering into negotiations with the parties internal to the organization.

2. Commercial Negotiations: Such types of negotiations are conducted with external parties. The driving forces behind such negotiations are usually financial gains. They are based on a give-and-take relationship. Commercial negotiations successfully end up into contracts. It relates to foregoing of one resource to get the other.

3. Legal Negotiations: These negotiations are usually formal and legally binding. Disputes over precedents can become as significant as the main issue. They are also contractual in nature and relate to gaining legal ground.

Is Negotiation Necessary?

Negotiation, at times can be a lengthy and cumbersome process. By asking whether it is necessary, time may sometimes be saved and unnecessary compromise avoided. On occasions, a request to negotiate may best be met by pointing out that the party making the request has no standing in the matter. If a manager has the undoubted authority to act, making a decision rather than negotiating about it may be the best tactic.

Alternatively, there are cases in which the best response to a request or a claim is to concede it without argument. Why waste time negotiating if the other party has a good case and there are no adverse consequences in conceding? Unnecessary negotiation, followed, perhaps, by a grudging concession of the other party's claim, will lose all the advantage that might be gained with a quick unexpected yes.

An alternative to a simple yes or no when a difference of view occurs is to skip negotiation and proceed immediately to some form of third-party intervention. An alternative to a simple yes or no when a difference of view occurs, is to skip negotiation and proceed immediately to some form of third-party intervention. On the most formal basis, this might imply a decision to take a dispute to court : informally, two managers who quickly realize that they cannot reach agreement about a working problem may jointly agree to stop wasting time in argument and refer the matter to a senior manager for resolution.

It is good to follow the general rule:

Do not negotiate unless you have to—or unless you can obtain some direct or indirect advantage by doing so.

The whole process of negotiation can be broadly divided into 3 stages:

1. A preparation phase before the negotiation begins.
2. The actual process of negotiating.
3. The implementation and follow up of the agreement.

Prior to the actual interaction that leads to an agreement between various parties, the preparation for a successful negotiation process is essential. The achievement of the target has to be systematic and strategic move. This asks for a detailed and minute analysis. A manager needs to be clear about his perspective.

1. Evaluate Relative Strengths: Before embarking on negotiation there is a need to assess the party's relative strengths. This strength can be defined as the power to influence others so as to have an upper hand over the final outcome. Each side has certain bargaining power on the back of which the whole negotiating process can be carried. While weighing relative strengths, the judgment regarding four things is involved :

- The amount of authority that each party possesses to conduct negotiations and the ability of the parties to make decisions.
- The strength of each party to get sanctions or benefits that are unrelated to the matter under negotiation.
- The logic or equity in the arguments.
- The firm determination with which each party pursues its case.

2. Set the Objectives: While planning negotiations, an assessment of relative strength should be linked to the determination of objectives. Usually, the stronger one's position is, the higher the level of objective achievement is there. The passing of the agreement takes place depending upon three different possible settlement levels.

- The ideal or the best possible deal.
- The expected settlement level.
- The worst, though still just acceptable deal.

As a negotiator, one needs to identify the top line objectives, the best achievable outcome and the outcome that can be acceptable at the lowest level. It is vital to consider the other party's viewpoint as well as one's own. One objective of negotiations is to help the other party feel satisfied with the outcome and not to be too aggressive in the process.

3. Keep an Eye on the Other Side: For conducting successful negotiation, an eye on the other party's plans, strengths and weaknesses helps in deciding a winning strategy. What are the objectives of the other party ? The facts and arguments they are likely to put forward and their overall winning strategy, all this knowledge is useful for preparing on the underlying and unstated issues. Besides, exchanging factual data before negotiations helps in overcoming delays or confusions. Checking of the issue, detailed facts and arguments, exchanging details are all preparatory assessments.

4. Decision regarding the Style and the Scene: This is planning of more actual negotiation. The negotiations can be conducted in number of different styles. They can be discursive or brisk, formal or informal, assertive or persuasive. Depending upon the role and responsibility of the individual the expression of these styles differ. Besides, whom to involve in the discussion process and whom not to involve, is a crucial task. Minutest details like the location of the negotiation site, the seating arrangements, refreshments to be provided, documentation aspects all need special attention. Negotiations are surely affected by the style, pace and composition of the negotiating teams but equally important are the seating plans, breaks and conducting of the session itself. It is also useful to keep some record of the outcome of negotiations to ensure a common understanding.

5. Setting of the Agenda: It is important to chalk out a plan of action in advance to avoid misunderstandings and common errors. If a clear cut guideline regarding what is to be done is provided, a lot of time and effort can be saved. The agenda may be formal or informal. If the subject, scope and purpose are fixed in advance, confusion can be avoided. It is useful to remember that the progress of negotiation is influenced significantly by the first speaker. One way of securing a strong opening position is to volunteer a brief rehearsal of the background before full negotiations begin.

6. Leading your case: To win the maximum favour in negotiation, tactics have to be used to strengthen one's position during the bargaining process. Prior to introducing a new issue, its acceptability by the opposite parties need to be rated. Compromise and concession are the essential aspects of negotiation. Equally necessary is the attachment of conditions to the concessions. The use of emotion in negotiating should be avoided. At times during discussions, people start getting emotionally attached. It is professionally dangerous to rise to the bait of personal attack. There are occasions, when a controlled display of emotion may be beneficial. For this, the two conditions are, that the emotion must be sincere and its use should be a conscious decision, not an instant reaction.

It is advantageous for a good negotiator to be a good listner. The most common fault occurs in saying too much and listening too little. To keep the heaviness out, use of humour reduces the tension. Use of humour also avoids a confron-tational mode.

Experienced negotiators usually do not commit themselves to definite statements until they are confident that this will not prejudice their position. The art of reading between the lines help in avoiding perceptional errors.

7. Timing and Adjournments: The maximum time for which an individual can maintain continuous attention and involvement, is somewhere around two hours. Henceforth, while planning negotiations, thought needs to be given to the time-scale. The longest period for effective continuous negotiation is about two hours. For this the time allotted for presentation can be 15 to 20 minutes and ideal time for individual contribution at the beginning of the discussion is two to three minutes.

Breaks and adjournments are helpful revival from monotonus discussions. They provide time to consider progress or new proposals within the team and avoid rash decisions. It also helps in bringing an end to unconstructive and personalized arguments. Besides, during the adjournment sessions the parties can have an opportunity for informal and casual talks.

8. Arriving at an Agreement: The closer the negotiation comes to end, the more sensitively the discussion needs to be handled. While weighing the benefits of the agreement, besides immediate returns the quality of long–term relationships also should be the crux.

The final offer and agreement needs to be timed to coincide with the discussion which is positively constructive. Before finalizing, it is advisable to check that all the aspects in the deal have been taken care of, particularly dates for implementation, completion time and definition and meaning of each term. Ensure that both parties fully understand what has been agreed and get the confirmation in writing. Those issues that still remain unsolved can be carried forward for future negotiations.

9. Effective Implementation: Arriving at an agreement is not an end in itself. The purpose with which negotiations are carried is to reach an outcome or action. An agreement is not successful until it has been effectively implemented. Adequate information and explanation should be supplied to those who are affected or apply the agreement.

10. Handling Breakdown: It is not necessary that negotiations always prove successful. At times an agreement may not be achieved and this requires other arrangements. A contingency plan should be kept ready in case of failure of the negotiations. The major options for handling breakdowns are either to go ahead on your own and take a decision that is best or seek third party intervention.

The Mind and the Heart

In 1998, the National Basketball Association (NBA) owners initiated a 202-day lockout of players, resulting in a loss of about $1 billion for owners and about half a billion dollars in foregone salaries for basketball players. Fans were frustrated and disenchanted, and supporters and advertisers lost millions. In 1999, the members of the World Trade Organization met in Seattle, Washington to lower trade barriers. The members of the organization could not even agree on an agenda and the meeting was an utter failure.

During 1999, Belinda Clark handled about 200 job offers for nursing assistants, research scientists, and a number of other employees. All but about 10 of these candidates took the initial offer without attempting to negotiate for something extra or more. Clark was delighted, but puzzled. The job applicants apparently did not realize that the offers Clark made were just starting points. She says, laughing, "I don't say anything if they don't." (Clark 1999, 88)

These examples suggest that negotiating is not easy. This is a problem, considering that people negotiate in their personal and business relationships, within organizations, between companies, across industries, and among nations.

Furthermore, negotiations occur between two people and, in other cases—such as the World Trade Organization—hundreds of people. The variety of negotiation contexts presents special challenges for managers, who are required to demonstrate competencies in all of these contexts. This book is designed to improve managers' and executives' negotiation skills across a wide variety of situations.

The working definition of *negotiation* used in this book is "an interpersonal decision-making process by which two or more people agree how to allocate scarce resources." By this definition, it is difficult to imagine how people can get through a single day without negotiating.

Negotiation as A Core Management Competency

Effective negotiation skills are increasingly important for executives, leaders, and managers in the business world. There are five key reasons for this.

Dynamic Nature of Business

Mobility and flexibility are the dictates of the new world of work. The dynamic, changing nature of business means that people must negotiate and renegotiate their existence in organizations throughout the duration of their careers. The advent of decentralized business structures and the absence of hierarchical decision-making provide opportunities for managers, but they also pose some daunting challenges. For example, most people do not stay in the same job that they take upon graduating from college or receiving their MBA degree; furthermore, most people will not have the same job as their predecessor. These realities mean that people must continually create possibilities, integrate their interests with others, and recognize that there will be competition both within companies and between companies (see Sidebar 1-1). Managers must be in a near-constant mode of negotiating opportunities.

Sidebar 1–1. New Businesses and Careers

According to *Business Week* (Alderman, 1999), it is the "era of the employee," with the tightest labour market in 29 years. This means that employees are in a one-up position, and employers need to keep them happy. For example, Doug Ross, the owner of Evolution Film & Tape Inc., a television production company in North Hollywood, California, lets his employees create their own hours, dress as they please, and bring their children to work—all in order to stay competitive. Employees and companies are in positions to negotiate all kinds of things, such as opportunities for training, flex time, family leave, health insurance, and other benefits. Another example: The California based Cheesecake Factory, Inc., pays salaries 20 percent above market rates. It also gives stock options to all its general managers, as well as new BMW 323s. This sounds expensive, but Cheesecake Factory says it has actually saved money, losing only two general managers in the last two years in an industry where a 38 percent turnover is the average (Conlin, Coy, Palmer, and Saveri 1999).

According to Linda Greene, associate vice-chancellor for academic affairs at the University of Wisconsin—Madison, "Many important events essential to professional success and professional satisfaction happen every day in the workplace and they are not always announced in advance" (Kalk 2000, 1E). In truth, negotiation comes into play when people participate in important meetings, get new assignments, head a team, participate in a reorganization process, and set priorities for their work unit (Kalk 2000). Ideally, negotiation should be second nature, but often, it is not.

Interdependence

The increasing interdependence of people within organizations, both laterally and hierarchically, implies that people need to know how to integrate their interests and work together across business units and functional areas. This not only occurs within companies, as people from different departments and units integrate their knowledge to create a product or service, but it also occurs between people from different companies, as is the case with strategic alliances. The increasing degree of specialization and expertise in the business world implies that people are more and more dependent on others to supply the components for a complete service or product. It is unwise to assume that others have similar incentive structures, so managers need to know how to promote their own interests while simultaneously creating joint value for their organizations. This requires negotiation.

Competition

Business is increasingly competitive. In today's economy, a few large firms are emerging as dominant players in the biggest markets. These industry leaders often enjoy vast economies of scale and earn tremendous profits. The losers are often left with little in the way of a market, let alone a marketable product (Frank and Cook 1995). This means that companies must be experts in the vast fields of competition. Managers not only need to function as advocates for their products and services, but they must also recognize the competition that is inevitable between companies and, in some cases, between units within a given company. Understanding how to navigate this competitive environment is essential for successful negotiation.

Information Age

The information age also provides special opportunities and challenges for the manager as negotiator. Computer technology, for example, extends a company's obligations and capacity to add value to its customers. This must be accomplished in a way that also benefits the company. Further, with ever-improving technology making it possible to communicate with people anywhere in the world, managers need to be able to negotiate at a moment's notice. Thus, the ability to determine relevant information from irrelevant information is critical for successful negotiation in the information overload age.

Diversity

Increasing diversity means that managers need to develop negotiation skills that can be successfully employed with people of different nationalities, backgrounds, and styles of communication. Thus, negotiators who have developed a bargaining style that works only within a narrow subset of the business world will suffer unless they can broaden their negotiation skills to effectively work with different people across functional units, industries, and cultures (Bazerman and Neale 1992). It is a challenge to develop a negotiation skill set generalizable enough to be used across different contexts, groups, and continents, but specialized enough to provide meaningful behavioural strategies in any given situation. This book provides the manager with such skills.

Most People are Ineffective Negotiators

Because negotiation is so important for personal and business success, it is rather surprising that most people do not negotiate very well—judging from their performance in realistic business negotiation simulations (for reviews, see Neale and Bazerman 1991; Thompson and Hrebec 1996; Thompson 1990a). For example, in a recent investigation of senior-level executives from major companies across the world, 95 percent reached suboptimal outcomes in a realistic business simulation; in practical terms, they "left money on the table."They are not alone. A voluminous body of evidence indicates that people consistently leave money on the table; walk away from profitable deals and in some cases, settle for something worse than they could otherwise obtain by pursuing a different course of action.

The Major Sins of Negotiation

There are four major shortcomings in negotiation we have observed and documented in our research. They are:

1. *Leaving money on the table* (also known as "lose-lose" negotiation) occurs when negotiators fail to recognize and exploit win-win potential.

2. *Settling for too little* (also known as "the winner's curse") occurs when negotiators make too-large concessions, resulting in a too-small share of the bargaining pie.

3. *Walking away from the table* occurs when negotiators reject terms offered by the other party that are demonstrably better than any other option available to them. (Sometimes this is traceable to hubris or overweening pride; other times, it results from gross miscalculation.)

4. *Settling for terms that are worse than your alternative* (also known as the "agreement bias") occurs when negotiators feel obligated to reach agreement even when the settlement terms are not as good as their other alternatives.

This book teaches you how to avoid these errors, create value in negotiation, get your share of the bargaining pie, reach agreement when it is profitable to do so, and quickly recognize when agreement is not a viable option in a negotiation.

Why are People Ineffective Negotiators?

The dramatic instances of lose-lose outcomes, the winner's curse, walking away from the table, and the agreement bias raise the question of why people are not more effective at the bargaining table if negotiation is indeed critical for business success. The reason is not due to a lack of motivation or lack of intelligence on the part of negotiators. Many of the managers who fall victim to the major sins of negotiation do so for three primary causes: absence of feedback, satisfying, and self-reinforcement.

Absence of Relevant and Diagnostic Feedback

Most people have little opportunity to learn how to negotiate effectively. The problem is not lack of experience but a shortage of timely and accurate feedback. Even those people who have daily experiences in negotiation receive very little feedback on their negotiating effectiveness. The absence of feedback results in two human biases that further prevent negotiators from optimally benefiting from experience. The first problem is the *confirmation bias,* or the tendency for people to see what they want to see when appraising their own performance. The confirmation bias leads people to selectively seek information that confirms what they believe is true. Whereas the confirmation bias may seem perfectly harmless, it results in a myopic view of reality and can hinder learning. A second problem associated with the absence of relevant and diagnostic feedback is *egocentrism,* which is the tendency for people to view their experiences in a way that is flattering or fulfilling for themselves. This may increase a manager's self-esteem; however, in the long-run, it does a disservice to managers by preventing them from learning effectively. For example, it was egocentrism and the corresponding inability to recognize her own shortcomings that lead to the removal of Jill Barad as chairperson/CEO of toy maker Mattel Inc. (Byrne and Grover 2000). According to analysts, Barad never assumed responsibility for earnings surprises or adverse announcements. Instead, she blamed her subordinates and sacked them.

Satisficing

The second reason why people often fall short in negotiation is due to the human tendency to satisfied (Simon 1955). *Satisfying* is the opposite of *optimizing:* In a negotiation situation, as we will argue later in this book, it is important to optimize one's strategies by setting high aspirations and attempting to achieve as much as possible; in contrast, when people satisfied, they settle for something less than they could otherwise have. Over the long-run, satisfying (or the acceptance of mediocrity) can do one's self and one's company a disservice because there is a variety of effective negotiation strategies and skills that can be cheaply employed to result in dramatic increases in profit (we will discuss these strategies in detail in the next chapters).

Self-reinforcement

The final reason why people perform poorly in negotiation is due to a principle known as *self-reinforcement,* which is the reluctance to try something new or change certain behaviours. It works like this: People are reluctant to change their behaviour and experiment with new courses of action because of the risks associated with experimentation. In short, the fear of losing keeps people from experimenting with change. Negotiators instead rationalize their behaviour in a self-perpetuating fashion. The fear of making mistakes may result in a manager's inability to improve his or her negotiation skills. In this book, we remove the risk of experimentation by providing several exercises and clear demonstrations of how changing one's behaviour can lead to better results in negotiation.

Debunking Negotiation Myths

Before we start on our journey toward developing a more effective negotiation strategy, we need to dispel several faulty assumptions and myths about negotiation. These myths hamper people's ability to learn effective negotiation skills and, in some cases, reinforce poor negotiation skills. In the following section, we expose the four most prevalent myths about negotiation behaviour.

Myth 1: Good Negotiators are Born

A pervasive belief is that good negotiation skills are something that people are born with, not something that can be readily learned. This is false because most excellent negotiators are self-made. In fact, there are very few naturally gifted negotiators. We tend to hear their stories, but we must remember that their stories are *selective,* meaning that it is always possible for someone to have a lucky day or a fortunate experience.

This myth is often perpetuated by the tendency of people to judge negotiation skills by their car-dealership experiences. Whereas purchasing a car is certainly an important and common type of negotiation, it is not the best context by which to judge your negotiation skills. The most important negotiations are those that we engage in every day with our colleagues, supervisors, co-workers, and business associates. These relationships provide a much better index of one's effectiveness in negotiation. In short, effective negotiation requires practice and feedback. The problem is that most of us do not get an opportunity to develop effective negotiation skills in a disciplined fashion; rather, most of us learn by doing. As the second myth reveals, experience is helpful, but not sufficient.

Myth 2: Experience is A Great Teacher

We have all met that person at the cocktail party or on the airplane who boasts about his or her great negotiation feats and how he or she learned on the job (Bazerman and Neale 1992). It is only partly true that experience can improve negotiation skills; in fact, naïve experience is largely ineffective in improving negotiation skills (Thompson and DeHarpport 1994).There are three strikes against natural experience as an effective teacher. First, in the absence of feedback, it is nearly impossible to improve performance.

For example, can you imagine trying to learn mathematics without ever doing homework or taking tests? Without diagnostic feedback, it is very difficult to learn from experience. The second problem is that our memories tend to be selective, meaning that people tend to remember their successes and forget their failures or shortcomings. This is, of course, comforting to our ego, but it does not improve our ability to negotiate. Finally, experience improves our confidence, but not necessarily our accuracy. People with more experience grow more and more confident, but the accuracy of their judgment and the effectiveness of their behaviour do not increase in a commensurate fashion. Overconfidence can be dangerous because it may lead people to take unwise risks.

Myth 3: Good Negotiators Take Risks

A pervasive myth is that effective negotiation necessitates taking risks and gambles. In negotiation, this may mean saying things like "This is my final offer" or "Take it or leave it" or using threats and bluffs. This is what we call a "tough" style of negotiation. Tough negotiators are rarely effective; however, we tend to be impressed by the tough negotiator. In this book, we teach negotiators how to evaluate risk, how to determine the appropriate time to make a final offer and, more importantly, how to make excellent decisions in the face of the uncertainty of negotiation.

Myth 4: Good Negotiators Rely on Intuition

An interesting exercise is to ask managers and anyone else who negotiates, to describe their approach to negotiating. Many seasoned negotiators believe that their negotiation style involves a lot of "gut feeling," intuition, and "in-the-moment" responses. We believes that this type of intuition does not serve people well. Effective negotiation involves deliberate thought and preparation and is quite systematic. The goal of this book is to help managers effectively prepare for negotiation, become more self-aware of their own strengths and shortcomings, and develop strategies that are *proactive* (*i.e.,* those that anticipate the reactions of their opponent) rather than *reactive* (*i.e.,* those that are dependent upon the actions and reactions of their opponent). Thus, excellent negotiators do not rely on intuition; rather, they are deliberate planners.

Learning Objectives

This book promises three things: First (and most important), reading this book will *improve your ability to successfully negotiate.* You and your company will be richer, and you will experience fewer sleepless nights, because you will have a solid framework and excellent toolbox for successful negotiation. However, in making this promise, we must also issue a warning: Successful negotiation skills do not come through passive learning. Rather, you will need to actively challenge yourself. We can think of no better way of doing this than to supplement this book with classroom experiences in negotiation, where managers can test their negotiation skills, receive timely feedback, and refine their negotiation strategies on a repeated basis.

Second, we provide you with a *general strategy for successful negotiation.* This book explicitly does not support a contextual model of negotiation, which prescribes using different negotiation strategies with different types of people, situations, and industries. Rather, we believe that negotiation skills are transferable across situations.

In saying this, we do not mean to imply that all negotiation situations are identical. This is patently false because negotiation situations differ dramatically across cultures and activities. However, there are key negotiation principles that are essential in all of these different contexts. The skills in this book are effective across a wide range of situations, ranging from complex, multiparty, multicultural deals to one-on-one personal exchanges.

Finally, this book offers an *enlightened model of negotiation.* Being a successful negotiator does not depend on your opponent's lack of familiarity with a book like this or a lack of training in negotiation. In fact, it would be ideal for you if your key clients and customers knew about these strategies. This approach follows what we call a *fraternal twin model,* which assumes that the other person you are negotiating with is every bit as motivated, intelligent, and prepared as you are. Thus, the negotiating strategies and techniques outlined in this book do not rely on "outsmarting" or tricking the other party; rather, they teach you to focus on simultaneously expanding the pie of resources and ensuring the resources are allocated in a manner that is favourable to you.

The Mind and Heart

Across all of the sections of this book, we focus on the *mind* of the negotiator as it involves the development of deliberate, rational, thoughtful strategies for negotiation. We also focus on the *heart* of the negotiator because it involves emotions, psychology, and the intuitive aspects of negotiation. This book strikes a balance between these two approaches to negotiation situations.

expanding the pie of resources and ensuring the resources are allocated in a manner that is favourable to you.

The Mind and Heart

Across all of the sections of this book, we focus on the mind of the negotiator as it involves the development of deliberate, rational, thoughtful strategies for negotiation. We also focus on the heart of the negotiator because it involves emotions, psychology, and the intuitive aspects of negotiation. This book outlines a balance between these two approaches to negotiation situations.

Index

A

All India Competitive examinations, 2

Ambassador of Australia, 88

Amin, Idi, 21

Andhra Pradesh, 2

Applying Multiple and Neuron Linguistic programmes, 8

Aryans, 49

Asian American Free Labour Association, 30

B

Bhakti (devotional), 58

Bodily-kinesthetic intelligence, 7

Boulwarism, 123

Brahma, 56

Brahman, 51

Buddha, 35

Buddhism, 35, 49

Buddhist clergy, 34

Business Week, 144

C

California based Cheesecake Factory, 144

Cambodian Constitution, 29

Cambodian Human Rights Coordination Committee, 39

Christianity, 58

Civil Rights Act, 63

Clark, Belinda, 142

Commercial negotiations, 136

Communication, 6

Compromise, 108

Computer technology, 145

Cultural relativism and universal human rights, 9-25
- argumentative cultural, 19-20
- assessing claims of cultural relativism, 22-23
- categorical cultural, 12-13
- conception of human rights, 17
- cultural relativity, 9
- cultural variation, 12
- culture and relativism, 18-19
- defining cultural relativism, 9-10
- evaluation of cultural, 15-16
- human mechanism, 12
- human rights, 23-24
- importance of relatives, 13-14
- justification of cultural, 22
- moral values of human rights, 14-15
- other views, 20-21
- recent trends in women rights, 24-25

relativism in implementing human rights, 16
relativity and universality, 11-12
rhetorical devices, 14
significance of cultural values, 13
universal rights, 17-18
varieties of cultural relativism, 15

D

Daniela any discourtesy, 106
Danish government, 36
Day-to-day/managerial negotiations, 136
Democratic empowerment of new government, 47
Deteriorating trends in humanities courses, 1-4
Determining the human excellence, 5-8
Doctrine of cultural relativism, 9

E

Electoral Component, 38
Enlightened model of negotiation, 152
Essentials of negotiation, 93-104
absence of relevant and diagnostic feedback, 98-99
competition, 96
debunking negotiation myths, 100
diversity, 97
dynamic nature of business, 94
experience is a great teacher, 101-102
good negotiators
are born, 100-101
rely on intuition, 102
good negotiators take risks, 102
information age, 96-97
interdependence, 95-96
learning objectives, 102-103
major sins of negotiation, 97-98
mind and the heart, 93-94, 104
most people are ineffective negotiators, 97
negotiation as a core management competency, 94
satisficing, 99-100
self-reinforcement, 100
sidebar 1-1. New businesses and careers, 95
why are people ineffective negotiators, 98

F

Franklin, Benjamin, 91
Fraternal twin model, 152
French government, 36

G

Gandhi, 59
Gardener, Howard, 6
Global citizenship, 85
Government of India, 88
Grand Master of Popular Education, Science and Traditional Culture, 20
Graphic Design units, 42

H

Haneef, Mohamed, 90
Hinduism, 49
Human nature, 12
Human rights and cultural values, 49-67

caste and the contemporary struggle for human rights, 62-67

caste in India, 49-62

caste, status and purity, 50-52

flexibility, mobility and equality, 56-62

human rights and traditional Indian society, 50

ontology of caste, 52-56

Human rights as education for peace, 68-87

development education, 81-82

environmental education, 85-87

peace education needs human rights education, 69-80

world order studies, 83-85

Human Rights Component, 30

Human rights education in unpeace building, 26-48

formal education, 32-34

informal education, 34-44

UNTAC human rights education mandate and strategy, 28-32

Human rights, national security and terrorism, 88-92

Humanities, 1

I

Indian University Campuses, 2

Inter Religious Mission, 35

International Committee of the Red Cross, 31

International Human Rights Law Group, 41

International Labour Organisation, 30

Inter-personal intelligence, 7

Interpersonal negotiation skills, 105-132

admit error and apologize, 126-127

avoid the presumption of evil, 115-116

avoid threats and manipulative tactics, 121-122

be tentative about reading people feelings, 128-129

break down bigger issues into smaller ones, 120

control emotions, 116-119

focus on the problem rather than the solution, 122-124

maintain integrity, 114-115

prepare, 112-113

reject weal solutions, 127-128

search for clarity, 113-114

separate problem from self-worth, 120-121

show patience, 114

try for interest-based solution, 124-125

understand time pressures, 119-120

Intra-personal intelligence, 7

Islam, 58

K

Kantian, 15

Keller, Allen, 34

Khmer Rouge period, 34

Khmer Rouge policy, 34

Knowledge and skills, 46

Kshatriya, 51

L

Legal negotiations, 136
Linguistic intelligence, 6
Logical mathematical intelligence, 6

M

Macias Nguema of Equatorial Guniena, 20
Madhya Pradesh, 1
Managerial negotiations, 133-141
  is negotiation necessary, 136-141
    arriving at an agreement, 140-141
    decision regarding the style and the scene, 139
    effective implementation, 141
    evaluate relative strengths, 137-138
    handling breakdown, 141
    keep an eye on the other side, 138-139
    leading your case, 139-140
    set the objectives, 138
    setting of the agenda, 139
    timing and adjurnments, 140
Manu, 55
Medical Faculty, 34
Mind and the heart, 142-153
Mind and the heart, 153
  absence of relevant and diagnostic feedback, 147-148
  competition, 145
  debunking negotiation myths, 149
  diversity, 146
  dynamic nature of business, 143
  experience as a great teacher, 150-151
  good negotiators
    are born, 149-150
    rely on intuition, 151
  good negotiators take risks, 151
  information age, 145-146
  interdependence, 144-145
  learning objectives, 151-153
  major sins of negotiation, 146-147
  most people are ineffective negotiators, 146
  negotiation as a core management competency, 143
  new businesses and careers, 144
  satisficing, 148-149
  self-reinforcement, 149
  why are people ineffective negotiators, 147
Ministry of Education, 33
Multiple Intelligence, 6
Musical intelligence, 7
Muslim, 49

N

National Basketball Association (NBA), 93
National Front for Construction and Defense, 35
National Labor Relations Board (NLRB), 123
Native American tribes, 18
Naturalist intelligence, 8
NBA, 142
Nepal, 58

NGOs, 30, 34
Nikhilanandra, Swami, 59

O

Orissa, 2

P

Paris Peace Agreement of October 1991, 28
Phnom Penh, 32
Placement and avenues, 2
Post-conflict peace-building, 27

R

Resolution, 112

S

Salvador, EI, 21
Sankritization, 57
Scheduled Castes, 63
Scheduled Tribes, 63
Scholarship, 2
Security council on Cambodia, 28
Security Council, 26
Shudra, 51, 60
Sikhs, 49
Spatial intelligence, 6
Sponsorship, 2
Supreme Court, 40

T

Task Force, 38
Third World, 24
Traditional Islamic social systems, 18
Trust Fund, 33

U

United Kingdom, 91
United Nations, 26, 35
United Nations Development programme (UNDP), 30
United Nations Education, Scientific and Cultural Organisation (UNESCO), 30, 36
United Nations in Cambodia, 28
United Nations Transitional Authority in Cambodia (UNTAC), 26
Universal Declaration of Human Rights, 12, 24, 70
Universal Human Rights, 9-25
University Grants Commission, 1
University of Wisconsin, 144
UNTAC Civil Administration Component, 40
Untied Nations Children Fund (UNICEF), 30

V

Vaishya, 51
Vietnamese, 35
Violence, 74

W

WATS (Pagodas), 35
World Conference on Human Rights, 38
World Trade Organization, 143
World Trade Organization, 94

Y

Yielding, 107
Yugoslavia, 75